THE

flower-powered
GARDEN

Supercharge Your Borders AND Containers
WITH Bold, Colourful Plant Combinations

ANDY VERNON

Timber Press
PORTLAND, OREGON

Published in 2018 by Timber Press, Inc.
The Haseltine Building
133 S.W. Second Avenue, Suite 450
Portland, Oregon 97204-3527
timberpress.com

Printed in China
Design by Cat Grishaver

Library of Congress Cataloging-in-Publication Data

Names: Vernon, Andy, author.
Title: The flower-powered garden : supercharge your borders
    and containers with bold, colourful plant combinations /
    Andy Vernon.
Description: Portland, Oregon : Timber Press, 2018. |
    Includes bibliographical references and index.
Identifiers: LCCN 2016055650 | ISBN 9781604696660
    (hardcover)
Subjects: LCSH: Flower gardening. | Flowers.
Classification: LCC SB404.9 .V47 2018 | DDC 635.9—dc23 LC
    record available at https://lccn.loc.gov/2016055650

ISBN 13: 978-1-60469-666-0

A catalogue record for this book is also available
from the British Library.

contents

introduction

I should begin by holding my hands up and admitting that when it comes to plants, I'm an addict. A plantaholic. A full-on floral and foliage fanatic. Guilty on both counts. But it gets worse. I'm obsessed with colour, too. I can't get enough of the stuff. I'd even confess that I may have a bit of a colour fetish. So in the summer, when bright and brash or deep and decadent blooms are blooming and lusciously coloured leaves are unfurling at full tilt, I get giddy.

I have to add, though: I can't really be blamed for this addiction. As a young boy, I spent a lot of time with my rather wonderful granddad, who also loved his blooms—and in particular, his bedding out. His pride and joy was a most amazing collection of regal pelargoniums. He grew them at the bottom of his backyard, in a curious building that was both my nan and granddad's outdoor bathroom and a sort of greenhouse cum potting shed. I can still smell that earthy, musty sweet scent it had. I loved to sneak inside and gaze at the impressive floral specimens, arranged on shelves and ledges around the bathtub. Granddad won lots of prizes for his regal pelargoniums at local horticultural shows. His passion for plants was much broader than just posh-sounding geraniums, however.

Granddad was a brilliant gardener with a flair for propagating all sorts of plants, which then filled up his various allotments and his backyard. He grew giant shrubby clouds of blue hydrangeas in big barrel pots at either side of the back door; standard fuchsias festooned with hundreds of dingle-dangle floral earrings; and hanging baskets overflowing with petunias, busy lizzies, coleus, and begonias. His numerous allotments were full of annuals and more-upright blooms for cutting, from dahlias, zinnias, and gaillardias to snapdragons and big shaggy China asters.

And as if all this weren't floriferous enough, Granddad and I would often walk to the park of a Sunday afternoon. On the way in, I would stop to admire the continual flutter of blue, green, and yellow budgies in the aviary near the entrance, but then we'd hurry on to take in the main event. The park's amazingly colourful beds

and borders were decked out in scarlet sage, purple cherry-pie-scented heliotropes, and plumes of feathery celosias; flossy blue ageratums circled tangerine tagetes, and busty tuberous begonias were hemmed in with white sweet alyssum, silver ragwort (dusty miller, to Granddad), and—of course—waves of navy blue lobelias. For an already flower- and colour-obsessed youngster like me, the formal park displays were a treat to visit and directly fuelled my own horticultural passions.

In retrospect, it's no wonder I still adore these vibrant, cheery, no-nonsense blooms. I like their kaleidoscopic colours, and their slightly bold and brassy attitude. I now enjoy visiting different sorts of gardens; I like sustainable perennial plantings, and I'm keen on hardy shrubs and trees and gardening for birds and bees. But sometimes it feels like the planting palette in our gardens and parks has become predictable, just a little too polite, and occasionally a bit boring. I find myself really missing the fearlessly floriferous plants of my granddad's world. They're the plants that, deep down, I truly revel in. However, in some haughty horticultural circles, my love of bedding blooms is a love that dare not speak its name. These plants are not trendy; they're deemed high maintenance, old hat, and they can be dismissed as unsustainable and a bit naff. This only makes me love and champion their outrageous, over-the-top, super-floriferous character even more.

Secretly I do sometimes wonder if it's a case of "the lady doth protest too much." Legions of dahlia lovers are finally holding their heads up high and coming out of the closet, so I'm convinced that there might be quite a few gardeners who, like me,

are proud to shout about their love of petunias, pelargoniums, and a whole raft of fabulous bedding blooms. I'm hoping they're all just waiting for the rebellion to happen and ready to march for an end to begonia bullying.

To me, bedding out is a welcome breath of fresh air. It's fun, it's frivolous, it's attention-grabbing, and it's super-colourful. That's its job, and its point. Every leaf and petal in a colourful bedding display emanates a sheer lust for life that fills me with energy and makes me feel pepped up and ready to take on the world. Surely that can't be a bad thing?

Back in its Victorian heyday, bedding out was all about floral pomp and circumstance and being over-the-top. Big displays were fabulous floral statements of grandeur and wealth, tended by lots of devoted gardeners showing off their cultivation skills and propagation prowess. The massively varied range of plant types included was all part of the performance. If you could grow it, you flaunted it—and bedded it out, parading those plants in front of an admiring audience.

Times and gardening fashions have changed hugely, and for me bedding out—though it is still about variety—should now be much more about quality, not quantity. Beds and borders carpet-bombed with battalions of identical begonias and edged with legions of lobelias and sweet alyssums are not for me. The best displays are intimate and joyous plant get-togethers, full of different leafy and blooming characters hobnobbing and hoofing it up in borders, window boxes, and containers, bringing fresh colour combinations and exciting floral themes to the plant party.

Clearly, in a more green and environmentally motivated world, bedding isn't the best option for huge expanses of land and doesn't even come close to being as sustainable as hardy perennial planting. But all plants can provide temporary leafy and floriferous microhabitats and pump out oxygen via photosynthesis in our small gardens, window boxes, baskets, and balconies. These are the places where we can all have some fun and grow gorgeous super-colourful plants that can really lift our spirits and green a little bit of the grey around us. More flower power and less concrete, please.

In my mind, whether we think they're fashionable or approve of their green credentials or not, the plants are having a grand old time, blooming their socks off and pursing their lips, pulling a floral "raspberry" at minimalist perennial planting schemes and shouting "Box balls!" in the direction of reliable evergreens. I'd like to think we are allowed to have just as much fun in our gardens and planting spaces as they are—teetering around in border displays, falling out of hanging baskets, and generally cavorting in containers. Well, that's how it looks to me.

Join the revival

I think it's time to right a wrong. To re-embrace the original playful, frivolous, and over-the-top Victorian spirit and variety of marvellous blooms and super-colourful bedded-out plant displays in our parks, gardens, patios, balconies, and containers. To grow the classless, hardworking, everyday, quick-to-cultivate, and floriferous plants that unfurl their leaves and bloom their hearts out like their very life depends on it. To celebrate the generous, easy-to-find, easy-to-please, easy-to-grow, supercharged flowers and foliage that just don't get the attention or appreciation they deserve. They should be welcome visitors in all gardens, big and small. To me, they are the "horticultural happy crowd" of the plant world. They have instant impact, and they are courageously colourful. They can be bold and brash but also dainty and delicate—that all depends on us, our choice of blooms and colours, and how we use them.

These plants arrive on the scene with attitude, make an immediate display, bang out blooms for weeks and weeks, and splish-splash colour around any outdoor space. Whether it's in established beds and borders, pots and patios, balconies and baskets, corridors and containers, they infuse any area with colour like it's raining flowers. They are plants growing at full throttle and pumping out pure colour and floral F.U.N. (Flamboyant Unbridled Nourishment) for the soul.

Bedding plants and bedding out

Traditionally these plants are known as bedding plants, but there is actually no such thing as a "bedding plant"—there are just plants. Furthermore, any plant that you place or plant outside temporarily in a bed, border, or container is effectively being "bedded out." It's far more about how you use the plant than what it actually is. So overall we are singing in a very broad happy-clappy church of plants that embraces one and all. These days, it's a rather eclectic and joyful mix of a large, committed, and quite traditional congregation with a constant stream of newcomers and a healthy sprinkling of born-again bloomers. Hallelujah.

Many of the plants that I like to use most, those that were traditionally bedded out, are tender. They need warm temperatures if they are to grow well and bloom; they will not withstand very cold weather or frosts. Often this is because they derive from species that originate in hot climates; in their native habitats, they can carry on growing from one year to the next, but in cooler, temperate climates, they tend to last just one long summer season. So, more often than not, they're planted out a few weeks after the last of the spring frosts, and after a long warm sunny blooming season, the show is brought to a close by cold wet winter weather. Begonias, petunias, and salvias are good examples.

Some colourful hardy and half-hardy annuals (plants that naturally complete their life cycle in one calendar year) are also very useful in displays. If given warmth and good light, these plants are super-quick, and in just a few months can go from seedy zero to flowery bloom-tastic. This is the case for popular plants like sunflowers, marigolds, cosmos, and nasturtiums. Again, these are the plants that really don't hang around once conditions are unfavourable.

More and more, the plants that I like to bed out are perennials. A few—such as colourful-leaved heucheras or zingy green euphorbias—are relatively hardy, lasting outside from one year to the next. Most, however, are short-lived or half-hardy perennials that either run out of floral steam after a couple of years and become a little

rangy and unkempt, or struggle to get through cold wet frosty winters. Often they are quite easy to propagate (from seed, cuttings, or by division) and relatively quick to mature into a fully blooming plant.

Tender perennials require a higher level of protection from the extremes of cold and wet weather to get them through winter—ideally, a gently heated greenhouse. Some, like fuchsias, can be rested in cool but frost-free, airy conditions, where they'll remain in complete floral hibernation mode through the darkest months. Others, like pelargoniums, can be brought inside, old leaves removed, and plants given a general tidy and placed behind glass—cared for a bit like a sleepy houseplant in a cool but frost-free unheated spare room or porch and kept very much on the dry side, too.

Cannas and other fleshy exotic plants can be dug up, cut back, and dried off slightly. If their roots are packed in moist but not wet compost and kept cool but totally frost-free, they can be successfully stored over winter and then planted out again the following spring.

In my garden, I bed out all sorts of wonderful spring biennials, bulbs, and perennials, while also giving a nod to some hardy and half-hardy flowering shrubs, textural grasses and sedges, brightly floriferous alpines, and awesome-leaved evergreens. So my approach to bedding out draws on an incredibly diverse range of plants, and that is pretty much the key. It's about mixing up all these plants and using them with a bit of frippery and flair throughout the year. Although many of my favourites are traditionally called "bedding plants," I think it's time to move on from this tired old term and liberate these wonderfully ornamental subjects. Let's celebrate their combined beauty and unadulterated passion for bringing life-affirming colour and joy into our private gardens, window boxes, terraces, public parks, and shared spaces.

And above all, let's remember what's so special and exciting about these displays. *They are temporary!* Meaning there are endless opportunities to rip up the rule book, experiment, and reinvent—the location, the containers, the colour scheme, the plants. Whether you want one long ever-evolving colour theme, or to design separate spring and summer idylls and maybe even cap it all off with a shorter hardier autumn/winter scheme—well, that's all up to you. This is set dressing for your garden, an opportunity not only to create your own floral spectacular but to tweak or totally change it whenever you want.

For me, always, it's all about the display as a whole, its overall flower power or blooming marvellousness, you might say. The intensity or subtlety of colours, singularly and in combination, is key, as are the clever associations and contrasts of the different sizes, shapes, and growth habits of the flowering and foliage plants. My favourite displays often include an element of the unexpected—whether that means the total reinvention of a much-loved or -maligned plant, or the incorporation of unusual colours, plants, materials, and containers. The best gardeners embrace experimentation and showmanship; ideally, they have a sense of humour and don't take themselves too seriously.

I hope I can inspire and encourage. I want to share with you some of the displays that I love, and the colour recipes and planting themes that I feel can work a treat. I've selected the likeliest plant players and, in the colour planting themes, some specific varieties to achieve the best effects, so you can get the same look if you want to follow a scheme and try it out. However, the idea is that you will have a go yourself. Let my examples be what spurs you to go for it: follow through with your own thoughts and feelings on colours and plant combinations. It's time to nurture your inner flower-mojo and leave traditional notions of bedding behind.

Flower-powered displays can be anywhere from surprisingly affordable to incredibly cheap, especially if you have the time to grow some plants from seeds and cuttings. The vast majority of these plants are also available early in the growing season as inexpensive plugs from all sorts of DIY superstores, garden centres, and nurseries; later on, they're sold fully grown, bursting into bloom, and garden-ready. This is "no-guilt gardening" for the time-poor. If circumstances are such that you need to garden in a much more "instant" way—and more and more, I do too—then let's drink to that and enjoy every gorgeous drop of colour, because these are the plants that are here to make us all feel good. Whatever your gardening space or budget, whatever your stock of free time, there are options that will work for you.

So let's have fun, go forth, and experiment. Most of all, let's flower-power our gardens and plant up our temporary flower and foliage displays with colourful, creative confidence. Be bold, be joyous, be blooming marvellous.

reinventing bedding displays

If you feel you're a bit lacking in inspiration or just a little daunted by the prospect of freestyle and flower-powered bedding displays, then this chapter will help you out. It's not always easy to come up with something fresh or different, and I don't blame anyone for getting to the garden centre and being completely wooed, wowed, and won over by what happens to be in full flower and looking fabulous. I have many moments of total weakness in a big well-stocked nursery. If you're the sort of gardener who, having once spied a gorgeous plant, accidentally says aloud, "Well, we need to find a little spot for you now, don't we?" (followed by worried looks from other customers), don't worry. I do it too. Even when I've got quite a clear idea of what I want to achieve in my head, sticking to a theme can be a challenge.

But have courage. Be bold. Enjoy yourself. Go for it. It's your garden or patio, your pots and troughs, beds and borders, boxes and baskets—your display. Too much holding back or too many compromises will often result in something you're just not that happy with in the end.

Explore and experiment with your favourite colours, flowers, and foliage. Knock yourself out and make it marvellous. This is a new world, where there is no shame in being over-the-top. We're not to blame. We're just common garden-variety flower fanatics, going about our business.

Shake off tradition

Times have changed, and so have the plants. We need to catch up with them. The range and types of plants for bedding out have moved on massively. They are expertly bred and super-colourful, and they bloom robustly. Many of the old issues that may have put you off in the past have been taken on and conquered by plant breeders. For example, most modern petunias are no longer rangy, straggly plants with flowers that don't stand up to wet weather; they are well branched, compact, floriferous, and relatively rain-resistant. Just like us, I'm pretty sure they want to be free from their past and allowed to live a little and let their hair down.

Sometimes we can feel a bit hemmed in by the history and heritage of bedding out. We think there's a certain set, regimented, formal style that plants must be planted in—straight rows, equidistant grid-like formations, carpet-like blocks of colour. Anything else feels a bit uncomfortable because it's not what we're used to, or it isn't what's gone before or what our mum and dad or nan and granddad did.

But deciding which plants to use in a display is all about the look *you* want to create. Have a good look at the different shapes, sizes, and forms of flowers and leaves, and tune in to the overall feel and atmosphere of a plant. Dwarf, well-branched, uniform, and upright varieties have a much more formal feel than taller, floppy-petalled, large-blooming, lax, trailing, and spreading ones. I always think looser, larger, and leafier feels much more relaxed and informal than compact, small, and super-floriferous. Don't be afraid, however, to mix together plants with very different habits and forms; this increases the variety and contrast within a display. In a display that has a simple or monochromatic colour theme, these extra layers of complexity—of plant habit and flower and leaf form, shape, texture, and size—are especially crucial.

Try putting things together in a looser, more contemporary style that suits you and your space. Mix things up. Make plant combinations. Or alternatively, in a very modern minimalist space, take just one colour or perhaps a particular plant variety, and try something very subtle, simple, and elegant, with lots of foliage to add impact.

Open your eyes

Having the confidence or skill to do something a bit more edgy or unusual with bedding plants and displays isn't going to come naturally to everyone. For me, the key to pulling off a really eye-catching, stylish, and well-executed display is combining either bright and bold or quite subtle and sophisticated colours. And the clues to a successful new colour combination often lie right underneath our noses, even within the plants themselves.

At first glance a flower might just seem . . . red. The more you look at it, however, the more you start to notice that its centre is in fact much darker, almost a sort of cranberry or plum colour, with a tiny yellow eye and some small black blotches. You then notice how the petals seem to glow slightly at the tips—that at that point, they are actually brighter, more of a vermilion that's edging towards orange. Then there's the dust-like pollen, a deep golden yellow, carried on the ends of creamy primrose-coloured filaments. On the back of the bloom, the petals are really deepest aubergine, and the stems atop which each flower sits appear to be a rich chestnut-brown when backlit by the sun. On closer inspection, the leaves aren't merely green; they're more emerald, quite shiny, and almost metallic, whereas the young shoots in the axils of the leaves are a vivid, crisp apple green.

So from the careful observation of just a single flower or leaf, a complex colour scheme of tints, tones, and shades along with contrasting and complementary colours is revealed right before your eyes. It's always worth taking a minute or more to stop and drink in a flower. When you do, all its differences will slowly become apparent. If they don't, have a glass of wine and have another go.

Once you start tuning in and observing colour in this way, colour combinations will come to you all the time. I find food and drink is particularly good for inspiring colour schemes—puddings, ice creams, cakes, cocktails, fruit sundaes. Places too have their own colour schemes, and armed with a digital camera or a smartphone, you can capture the hidden colour language going on around you by taking pictures of

The colour wheel.

all the different quirky things in your location. Schemes are everywhere, all around us, in the most random everyday things—tree bark, a fallen leaf, the wrapping on a pack of sweets, funky wallpaper, a street poster, the clouds at sunset, the pattern in a woolly jumper. In front of our eyes at this very moment. Start looking that little bit closer, and they'll reveal themselves.

Know the colour basics

At heart I'm a firm believer in learning the rules, understanding them and their limits. But then, after you've done this, it does make it that much more fun to have a good go at contradicting them, by experimenting and seeing how far you can push colour combinations. This is when the real fun begins. But to feel confident using colours when designing planting combinations for bedding displays, it can really help to first understand some of the basics of colour theory, and the difference between the various terms used to describe colours: hue, shade, tint, and tone.

- A hue is an original, pure foundation colour. We may refer to various types of red—claret, scarlet, burgundy—but the true, pure colour, or hue, is red.

- A shade is a pure colour (or hue) with a degree of black added to darken it. Shades can add depth, drama, weight, and atmosphere to a scheme.

- A tint is a pure colour (or hue) with a degree of white added to lighten it. Tints brighten or accentuate a particular colour, helping it to pop and stand out.

- A tone is a pure colour (or hue) with a degree of grey (both black and white) added—effectively, the hue toned down. Tones can be really useful, adding extra richness and variety to the lighter tints and darker shades.

Break out the sunglasses and the tequila. This flower show competition display celebrates both the Mexican Day of the Dead and the national flower of Mexico, the dahlia. It's bright and bold, packed with dazzlingly vibrant colour.

The primary colours are red, yellow, and blue; when combined, these make the secondary colours, orange, purple and green. The mix of primary and secondary colours, or the sort of overlapping areas, are often called tertiary colours. This is where it all starts to get much more interesting. The tertiary colours are amber (yellow-orange), chartreuse (yellow-green), vermilion (red-orange), magenta (red-purple), violet (blue-purple), and teal (blue-green).

Those are just a few basics of what's quite a complex subject. We often describe colours and the effects that they have on and with each other in simple terms and in an idealised way, and we think solely about the colour (or hue). But there's much more going on. Lightness (how light or dark the colour is) and saturation (how intense or dull the colour is) add to the complexity and sophistication of a bedding colour scheme. Opposite-coloured blooms will intensify each other when they are sited right next to each other. The thing to be wary of is combining a variety of different blooms in lots of opposing pure, vibrant hues, resulting in a full-on floral fistfight of colour. I admit the devil in me rather loves and laughs at this, but even I will need a sit-down, a stiff drink, or a large pair of sunglasses—ideally all three—if I look at them for too long. But do have fun with the complexity of colour. Play around with it and try things out. The possibilities are really endless, and if it all gets a little bit clashy and super-crazy-colourful, well, don't worry too much. Everyone tends to look good in big sunglasses.

THINK PINK

You may notice one incredibly popular colour of bedding flowers has not yet been mentioned. It's pink, it's everywhere, and it totally fascinates me.

Pink doesn't quite fit with scientific explanations of colour. There is, after all, no pink in the colours of the rainbow. Some scientists argue that pink is a combination (or versions) of red and violet, two colours, which, if you look at a rainbow, are on opposite sides. Their conclusion? Since it cannot occur in nature without bending the colours of the rainbow to allow red and violet to commingle—which, apparently, is theoretically impossible—pink doesn't actually exist.

However, we all know that pink can be mixed by putting red, blue, yellow, and white paints or pigments together. Confused? Me too.

Essentially, when we see any one of the many subtly different colours we call pink, we're seeing red or violet that has either a slight yellowness or a slight blueness to it. What we all think of as a distinct colour or hue is in fact a very complex mix of reflected light. When we look at a pink flower or leaf, we are not actually seeing pink wavelengths of light as such, but a mixture of other colours of light being reflected as other wavelengths are absorbed. There are pinks that appear much more red (hot, cherry, or cerise pinks), some that appear more violet or blue (fuchsia and magenta pinks), and some that feel quite close to orange or yellow (apricot, peach, and coral pinks). I can find pure joy in most.

Mix up your palette

Classic, well-tested colour recipes are a great starting point for any plant display. Combining colours is a bit like many things—running, camping, baking, kissing. The more you do it and get into it, the better you get at it and the more you like it. So have a go and before you know it, your confidence will grow and there'll be no stopping you. You'll be flying—cooking up and flirting with colour themes to your heart's content.

A SINGLE MINGLE

One of the easiest colour themes to execute well is a monochromatic display. At its simplest, you are choosing a single colour and putting together a display that exclusively features blooms of this pure single hue. It can be surprisingly effective. An ultra-simple interpretation is to find an amazing flowering plant you love and use just that variety with a bold foliage plant, so showcasing a particular bloom with a leaf that echoes the colour. For a more layered and interesting display, add variety by choosing plants that have flowers of different sizes and shapes, in different tints, tones, and shades of the chosen colour. You may also want to pick out foliage plants that echo this colour in the variegation of their leaves. Keeping things clear, defined, simple, and straightforward can produce very striking, sophisticated, and dramatic displays.

Monochromatic white.

This yellow and purple complementary display in downtown Chicago uses two opposite colours to great effect.

OPPOSITES ATTRACT

A second simple but classic colour theme uses just two complementary colours, colours that are total opposites. Blue and orange, red and green, yellow and purple. Any two colours that face each other directly across the colour wheel. Blue lobelias with orange marigolds; red pelargoniums with lime green nicotianas; purple petunias with rich yellow dwarf sunflowers—simple examples of total opposites perfectly complementing each other. In these schemes, each colour has a powerful effect on its opposing partner. They supercharge and intensify each other, and overall the visual effect is even stronger. There's lots of room to play within these combinations, as with each colour, you can choose from pale gentle pastel tints and tones to bright super-saturated hues or deep dark intense shades, and everything in between. So you may actually have four or five quite different types of plants, with a range of orange blooms, contrasting with, say, a similarly varied suite of blue-flowered plants, giving the whole display more interest and variety.

Red and green are two classic opposite colours that intensify each other in this simple complementary scheme.

Split complementary colour schemes feature a colour combined with the two colours on either side of its natural opposite. So instead of choosing red to go with green, green is paired with the colours that occur on either side of red on the colour wheel, red-orange (vermilion) and red-purple (magenta).

This small garden display has been put together using the same bold triad of primary colours—red, yellow, and blue.

CONTRASTING COLOURS

Choosing colours from all around the colour wheel that are equidistant from each other can create some great contrasting colour themes. The primary colours red, yellow, and blue make a bold triad combination, as do the secondary colours orange, purple, and green. All six tertiary colours—amber (yellow-orange), vermilion (red-orange), magenta (red-purple), violet (blue-purple), chartreuse (yellow-green), and teal (blue-green)—work really well together, too. Plants such as ornamental sweet potato (*Ipomoea batatas*) are great for adding a real chartreuse or acid green; for teal, certain hostas, agaves, or succulents with a bluish bloom to their leaves can do the same. Alternatively, you could let containers with a chartreuse, teal, or amber glaze do the work of adding those particular tertiary colours to an adventurous colourful scheme.

This mix of calibrachoas uses the three primary colours to full effect. Each makes the others that little bit more impactful.

HARMONIOUS COLOURS

As well as using opposing or complementary colours effectively, gorgeously colourful displays can be made by using colours that are close neighbours on the colour wheel. Classic combinations include warm yellows, amber, orange, and vermilion, or a collection of the cooler colours, such as purple, violet, and blue. Any small arc or section of the colour wheel can be used to put these together. In some ways, this is just like taking a scheme featuring one single colour and welcoming in the harmonious colours on either side to add more variety.

A favourite harmonious combination of mine is strong powerful orange with hot pinks and intense magenta—really, all the vibrant neighbours of red on the colour wheel. These fruity colours make my mouth water, and I never seem to tire of them. You don't need to limit yourself to just the pure hues, however. Always make full use of all the tints, tones, and shades of the colour group to bring more depth and excitement to your display.

Cooly harmonious.

Warmly harmonious.

One of my personal favourite colour schemes is to use vibrant pinks, reds, oranges, and yellows together, creating a tropical and fruity mix.

MULTI-MARVELLOUSNESS

Multicoloured, rainbow, or polychromatic displays can seem easy to put together, appearing as they do to be simply full of absolutely every colour in the book. If you study them a little further, however, the best ones are significantly more clever. Some exclude one or two key colours. Others pick out a particular hue and emphasise it that little bit more, to give the overall multicoloured display a warm glow, a lively contemporary zingy twist, or a cool sophisticated edge. Others stick to soft pale pastel tones, or bring together a wide group of deep dark rich shades. Those that combine lots of fully saturated hues can be positively energising but sometimes a little exhausting, giving the impression of a colour fight in full swing.

Keep an eye on the balance of warm and vibrant (colours like yellows, oranges, hot pinks, and reds) to cool and calming (blues, greens, purples, and mauves). Mixtures of intense saturated shades and bright hues can feel powerfully punchy and vibrant together, whereas a selection of pale pastel tints and tones helps create a gentle, relaxed mood. Or perhaps a more vintage, chocolate-box, or in-an-English-country-garden effect is what you're after; if so, choose plants with blooms in hues and pastels from around the colour wheel, but be sure to season it all with a dainty sprinkling of white-flowering plants. This type of mixture can often give a traditional or "cottagey" feel to a display. Add a thatched roof, oak beams, lime-washed walls, and a small army of jolly hanging baskets if you feel like going the whole hog.

The devil is in the colour details. Getting the right amount of each colour in your selection of plants, and placing, mixing, and layering them together in the display, can be quite an art. There is always a huge amount of fun and a slight element of luck involved in getting everything just right in a multicoloured display.

This multicoloured display has a dramatic dark-leaved dahlia, whose yellow flowers echo the burnt orange and warm rusty colours in the coleus, as its main focal plant throughout. Other plants inject purples, pinks, reds, and greens.

This display in a downtown Chicago plaza features strong hues and tones of magenta, pink, yellow, bronze, and red—and all sorts of greens. Overall, its multi-layered richness feels vivid and energised.

GREEN, GLORIOUS GREEN

Within any plant display, mono- to polychromatic, the role of foliage is pivotal to the mix. Green is often the common colour thread, the reason many planting combinations and schemes featuring fierce, clashing, and opposing colours—which really shouldn't work well in theory—look good in a garden situation; green in all its tints, tones, and shades is often the magic that helps make these challenging colour combinations and themes blend that little bit better. Leaves have a calming and harmonising effect amongst all the colourful flowers, knitting a whole display together, and green is just the start of the story. Leaves clearly aren't just providing one colour. They can be almost jet black, chocolate brown, bronze, silver, grey, pewter, lime, acid yellow, and even olive and orangey green, plum red to burgundy green, bluish—and that's just talking colour. The most memorable displays and planting combinations have lots of foliar colours and textures enhancing their effectiveness. The range of forms, shapes, sizes, and textures is incredible and—what with all the different patterns and veination—marvellously mind-blowing. If a new bedding scheme you've devised isn't quite working, it's worth looking to green and thinking about adding more foliage plants into the mix to help calm or complement the overall colour effect you're trying to achieve.

Similarly, if the colours of blooms are clearly clashing that bit too much, try incorporating some green-flowering plants, like *Nicotiana* 'Lime Green', into a scheme. It amazes me how often this saves a bedding colour scheme that's not quite working. Swapping ever-popular but often-overused white blooms for green ones in a colour theme can also have a dramatic and interesting effect on a bedding display.

WILFUL WHITE

I always tread very cautiously with white. Many people would say that white is calming, gentle, subtle, and relaxing. It's true that in many shady situations—and combined with an abundance of other gentle off-whites, greens, and silvers—this can be the case. However, white can also be the brightest, most aggressive and attention-grabbing "colour" of all. Forget hot pink and canary yellow—pure white shouts loudest. It reflects all colours of light, so given enough sunshine it can soon be too much, too bright, and before you know it, it's positively glaring, overpowering and dominating a display. In the worst-case scenario, you get a whitewash effect, where the bright white blooms dazzle and take over, diluting the effect of all the other colour combinations.

My advice is to always place white-flowering plants sparingly in any scheme but especially in very bright sunny locations. Increasingly I choose pale off-whites and gentle blush pastels rather than dazzlingly pure white blooms—and temper it all with some green-flowering varieties, too.

These themed planters in pinks, mauves, and blue illustrate how big white blooms can shout too loud and dominate a planting combination. Always use white sparingly.

Bedding schemes made up of purely strong colours, without any white at all in them, often instantly feel more contemporary, bold, and modern, whereas a lot of white in a display lends an old-fashioned, almost Granny-ish aura—particularly lots and lots of small white or traditional bedding blooms dotted throughout a scheme. But again, if you're going for a very vintage, cottage look, this may be exactly what you want.

Other aspects to consider when you are weighing the amount of white to include are weather resistance and general maintenance. Rain and damp can cause white blooms to mottle and turn brown rather quickly, whereas with richly coloured blooms the effects are much less noticeable. Even when the sun shines, white blooms frequently turn brown once they've gone over, and unfortunately the younger fresher flowers really tend to highlight the dead brown ones in the display, thus worsening the effect. In general, schemes containing lots of white blooms are more high maintenance, requiring more regular picking over and deadheading. Rich, intense, and dark-coloured blooms tend to keep their colour as the flowers finish, so the dead blooms are slightly less noticeable. Less white can mean less time and effort required for sprucing up a display during blooming season.

COLOUR TRICKS AND TREATS

The preceding discussions of terms, theories, and themes are not meant to form a "colour bible." In many ways, I'd rather love you to contradict the lot of these seeming rules, and experiment with all sorts of colour clashes. Outdoors there's so much green, so much sky, not to mention the many colours of brickwork, masonry, fences, pots, and containers. Basically, many elements other than plants contribute to the colours that make up the picture. Maybe this is why so many colour combinations that shouldn't ever work in theory often look great in reality. The colour rules often bandied about—"pink and yellow don't go well together," for example—have always been a red rag to a bull for me. Have fun and try them out for yourselves. Personally, I love a rhubarb and custard spring planting combination.

The trick: foliage plants like coleus (*Solenostemon*) and Persian shield (*Strobilanthes dyeriana*) bring long-lasting colour, incredible texture, and a dash of modernity to a display. The treat? They require less maintenance.

Warm colours like bright reds, oranges, pinks, and yellows will liven things up and often make a display feel more present and welcoming. It's like turning the heating on. The cool blues, greens, and purples essentially do the opposite; they will feel like they are retreating slightly, so you're taking your foot off the accelerator and calming things down. That's two of the simplest tricks you need to know about colour to get you going. It's amazing how quickly you learn about colour as you put together your displays each season.

Another trick is to take a fortnightly photograph when you're trying out a new colour scheme. Bedding displays grow quickly, and it's interesting to track the changes. Which plants grow the fastest, flower the longest, or need trimming and pinching out? Note things like which varieties overwhelm and try to take over, and which ones might struggle to compete. All this will dramatically affect the balance of the colours in the display. Sometimes you may have got the colour combinations right but just not used the right mix of plants. Comparing photos over time can really help to highlight what might need tweaking next time.

Finally, think carefully about the overall effect, the atmosphere, and the balance of colour that you want the flowers and foliage in your display to deliver. Totally bloomtastic displays are florally fabulous, but they can feel a bit old-fashioned, or ever so slightly over-the-top. Allowing the shapes, colours, and textures of foliage to play a greater role is a trick that can help any display look more fresh, modern, and contemporary. Leaves can still inject plenty of colour, and fewer flowers and more foliage might also mean a little less time is required for deadheading during the flowering season. In the end it all comes down to you; your own personal preference will determine your perfect balance. More and more, I'm increasing the number of foliage plants and deliciously scented aromatic-leaved plants in my displays as well as being more choosy about the flowering plants I use. And I'm loving the results.

Plan ahead and shop around

If you can get organised well in advance and have a plan for your display and stick to it, you will be able to save a considerable amount of money in the long run. Go online to find out where you can be sure to obtain some of your specific, unusual, or new varieties. There are bargains to be had ordering germinated seedlings and plug plants in advance on the Internet. Some of the extra-special new introductions may be exclusive to certain companies. If you order small plug plants in advance from specialist suppliers, then you can be pretty sure of getting exactly what you want and often get some great deals, too.

If you want to grow most of your own plants from seed, then autumn and winter is the season to get your orders in. Otherwise, head to the garden centre, beginning in early spring. Get to know your local nurseries and garden centres; explore the range of plants they stock, and when they stock them, and discover what plant bargains they offer. This is a particularly good idea if you're an instant gardener, so that you know where to go for a good selection. If you tend to hunt for most of your plants at mature or planting-out size, look for lush healthy young plants just about to come into flower. Try not to buy ones that are already in full bloom, as these may have been flowering for some time and their show may not last as long. Don't expect to get everything you need from just one garden centre or local nursery, especially if you leave things to the last minute. Keep to your colour plan, but be open to adjustments in terms of plant choice. There are usually lots of different plants that can deliver the colours you want in your scheme.

It pays to shop around; compare prices, plant size, and quality. Plugs and mini-plants are often a bargain, but you will need somewhere bright and frost-free to grow them on before planting out. Don't go mad and buy way more than you need (something I can't seem to help doing myself).

This dark wicker hanging basket complements the dark brown front door perfectly, and the orange, mustard, red, and terracotta of the blooms pick up on the colours in the brickwork, too.

I've found that being flexible on some plant choices when it comes to colour can save heaps in the long run. Don't compromise on everything, however, and particularly not the "star performers" in your scheme. If you have your heart set on a certain striped petunia or a stately canna with dramatic leaves, then go the extra mile to source it. I find the most distinctive displays usually hang off a few absolutely fabulous standout varieties.

If you really come unstuck tracking down must-have plants, then post comments and messages on gardening group pages and profiles on social media to mobilise armies of amateur gardeners to help you source and locate blooms. It could save you hours of time scrolling through websites.

Let your location lead the way

The location of a bedding display is an important element of it. One place where there's often lots of features that can influence or be incorporated into your plan is the front entrance to your home. Study the colours and textures of things like the brick, stone, masonry, roof tiles, driveway, gravelled areas, and woodwork, and—more importantly—the colours of painted features (e.g., front doors, porches, window frames, garage doors). There's an opportunity to weave some of these colours and textures into the theme, and make a display that feels really grounded, well thought through, and perfectly positioned.

There are lots of other locations around your home and garden that you may want to create a bedding display: verandahs, balconies, window ledges, decked areas, patios, beds, borders, and so on. Look carefully at what's already there, and consider the colours or textures of stained fencing, pergolas, garden sheds, garden gates, ironwork, garden ornaments, rusted plant supports, paving, paths, seats, and garden furniture. Take into account the colour theme of the permanent planting in the garden as a whole—trees and shrubs, wall- and fence-covering climbers, perennial plants that do their thing at pretty much the same time every year. Pulling out some of the present colours and themes and combining these in a bedding display will help anchor that display within a space. A temporary but stylish display can often add to the bigger picture hugely, by enhancing, highlighting, and complementing the existing features and plants.

This Mediterranean-themed display has used identical traditional terracotta pots in a very clever way. Some have been left plain, others painted in colours that contrast nicely with the blooms of the pelargoniums.

Something as simple as a rusted vertical plant support featuring the same white begonia in plain terracotta pots can be very effective.

Choose containers carefully

The more colourful and diverse the planting, the more elegant and understated the containers should be. Or to put it another way, the less fussy your pots, the more the attention stays on the plants in them. In my experience durable, sturdy, simple, and well-made pots in neutral and natural colours are best. Plain old aged-terracotta pots seem to work well in absolutely any situation; these familiar and uncomplicated pots allow the plants to be the stars.

Modern containers with interesting textures, often created from complex resins, can have the look and feel of stone and natural materials and be much lighter and easier to move around; buy the best-quality ones you can afford. Very large bold-coloured containers are a lot of fun but should be used sparingly and carefully for the best effect. Big contrasts in style and colour often work well if done with courage and confidence; however, before you spend a small fortune in the outdoor pots department of your favourite homeware store or garden centre, keep the style and overall design of your home in the front of your mind. Have you gone bold or big enough, or are the containers versatile enough to

use again and again? A group of just a few large pots often has far more presence and impact that a gaggle of smaller ones.

Consider too the pots, window boxes, or hanging baskets you already have. If you like to reuse things and get a good return on your garden centre purchases, it's good to build a collection of complementary containers, ones that give you the option to mix and match and use in various groupings and situations in the garden. On the whole, I avoid pots and containers with bold patterns, or ones that have prominent motifs, words and calligraphy, and fussy designs. I find them distracting and limiting, and besides, I want my pots and containers to be ultra-versatile.

Container choice can be key to executing a fresh and exciting display. It's good to have an overall theme that connects and unites them in a display, such as being made from the same material or having a similar finish: plain terracotta, glossy glazes, zinc, etc., or all belonging to a particular colour group. Often it's good to vary the sizes quite dramatically in a large display so you get a range of heights and shapes and options to place different pots in smaller subgroupings. Odd groups of just a few different-sized pots clustered around focal points in the garden can look wonderful.

With the addition of a drainage hole, an old teapot becomes a fun container for planting.

Repetition and careful spacing of the exact same container across a defined area can be incredibly effective. If that display also repeats the exact same plant or planting recipe, the effect is even more striking. Such a display oozes confidence and can work particularly well when planned as a vertical, using pots mounted on a wall, fence, or ladder.

Upcycling all sorts of quirky, preloved, everyday items can add your personality and individual flair to a display. Choose a common theme for the selection of upcycled items rather than just totally random things, and you will take a display into a whole new dimension of marvellousness. Be wary of using too many small or similarly sized containers: they may make a display feel cluttered. A broken chest of drawers, worn-out watering cans, old tin baths, cooking pots and saucepans, vintage biscuit tins, chimney pots, wine crates, tin cans, colanders, teapots, water troughs, oil drums, chairs, tyres, teacups and saucers—a quick Internet search for upcycled planters can inspire and amaze. I rather love the confidently kitsch and colourful ideas the most. Playful objects and plastic toys sprayed in very bright block colours with flowers popping out of them usually plant a big smile on my face, no matter how extraordinary or ever-so-slightly ridiculous.

Frame it

Before planting up any display, it's worth taking a step back and playing around with the placement of plants, as if you're composing a photograph. Visualize the ideal picture you are hoping to create, but try a few different things before committing plants or containers to their final positions. If the display is mainly made of containers and close to the house or a prominent focal point in the garden, it's especially important to get the balance right. Looking at the wider picture—and what's already in it—really helps when it comes to the overall design and layout of the display you're introducing. Consider every one of the existing features. You could decide to either balance or echo them by repeating tall or large substantial plants or big containers to create a sense of order, symmetry, or rhythm. Alternatively, you can contrast and accentuate the differences in sizes and heights and go for a more asymmetrical, abstract, or one-sided arrangement. Experiment with the number of plants or containers; the balance and position of thrillers ("spot" upright plants), spillers (sprawlers and trailers), and fillers in a scheme; or the number and size of pots, hanging baskets, and window boxes.

This pink, green, and white display is planted up in a range of containers, including an oddball assortment of plastic pots that were given a new lease of life: they were cleaned out, rubbed down with coarse sandpaper, and given a few coats of textured masonry stone-effect paint. Newly disguised, the cheap mismatched plastic pots now sit seamlessly amongst more elegant terracotta and glazed celadon containers.

Plant generously and variously

The displays that impress and wow me most are all about innovation, floral and foliage variety, and unabashedly joyous colour. "Too much," "over-the-top," "knockout"—these are actually all compliments in my book. Once they're up and running, displays should be nonstop sensations of leaves and flowers.

"Less is more" is not me, and I'm fine with that. I just don't buy it when it comes to flower power. Sadly I feel that "less" often really is just less these days. Less people finding the time to make an effort in their patch, fewer flowery front gardens, a decline in bees and butterflies, dull grassy traffic roundabouts, dead window boxes, and the disappearance of parks department nurseries, which used to grow bedding plants in the thousands to plant across our cities and towns. Less is not blooming more, because in the end we're just left with—less.

I think we should turn the tide on "less." More is almost always more. Protest with petunias, fight back with fuchsias, and fill front gardens, containers, patios, and window boxes with blooming colour. Be generous, plant as much and as many plants as you want. Freestyle

In my hometown of Crewe, the displays are often quite colourful and well intentioned if a bit old-fashioned. Here's a prescription to give our towns and cities a more modern twist: pick a colour theme and inject more plant variety.

Formal bedding out can look appropriate and tidy in the context of historic parks and civic centres.

bedding is all about variety—so join me in banging on my bedding revival tambourine and use plants any which way you want to.

Traditionally in parks and public spaces, plants like begonias, petunias, salvias, and pelargoniums are planted en masse. It's a bit like painting by numbers to create living floral carpets, with edging plants in strict lines and dot plants in the middle, but the result can feel very boring and slightly trapped in the past. I think we can have more fun with these plants, and our gardens are the perfect place to celebrate variety and diversity, to try out all sorts of new and different plants, and put them together in experimental ways. So out with carpets and in with interesting and fun combinations. It's more modern, too: grouping plants in mixed communities rather than massed monocultures is a healthier way to grow them.

Plant anytime, anyplace, anywhere

You don't need a devoted area of your garden to have fun with super-floriferous and leafy plants; they can fill any quirky or challenging planting space with instant colour and look good mixed into all sorts of garden situations. Add them to small semi-shady areas in need of a lightening, brightening lift of gentle colour, or areas of gravel, where sun-loving bloomers will break up the stony monotony and thrive. Ribbons of bold colour look wonderful wending through permanently planted beds in need of a colour infusion come high summer. Beds of annual climbers and taller bedding varieties can serve as temporary screens; shorter ones make dwarf hedges, to define and highlight specimen plants or an area of interest. Incorporate them across the garden to inject interest whenever and wherever it's lacking.

Visit trial grounds

Many breeders and producers of ornamental plants, seed and plant companies, and the organisations that trial and compare plants will hold spring and summer showcases at their trial grounds and show gardens.

Nurserymen, growers, garden centre and parks department staff, horticulture industry professionals, and the gardening media visit to see and spot the best varieties to grow or exciting new introductions to publicise. On a bright sunny day, these locations are super-saturated plant theme parks, a smorgasbord of colour that's totally bedazzling, and more and more they are open to the public on various days. If you can make time to visit, they are a brilliant way to compare similar varieties growing in standard garden conditions and discover brand-new ones. You can get a clear idea of the varieties that are coping best with recent weather conditions, view differences in height and spread, and get a feel for the most floriferous varieties and sometimes an inkling of the most pest- and disease-resistant ones, too. You can also really hone colour choices and observe subtle differences between cultivars; on paper and in pictures, some variations seem incredibly minor, but when the plants are growing and performing right next to each other, the shades of difference are much more obvious.

If pollinator-friendly and nectar-rich bedding plants are what you're after in particular, then given a bright sunny day, you will quickly pick up on the types and varieties visited the most by bees and insects—and the ones that they seem to completely ignore.

As well as the more formal trial areas featuring strips and blocks of plants, there are usually more exuberant display areas where varieties in hanging baskets, containers, planting pouches, modular living wall systems, and vertical towers are grown to perfection. Here it's good to spot the individual cultivars that stay compact, look best from below or above, are self-branching, trail beautifully, or perform the very best in a vertical wall (or whichever specific type of container they are grown in). It's an amazing source of tips and expert insider info as well as a brilliant day out for any flower fanatic. Don't forget your camera and notebook if you should get the chance to visit.

Trial grounds at Ball Colegrave Ltd.

Osteospermums now come in the most incredible colours, some with contrasting centres. This is *Osteospermum* 'Serenity Blue Eyed Beauty'.

Coleus offer an amazing range of colourful and intricate leaf markings. This is *Solenostemon scutellarioides* 'Fishnet Stockings'.

Robust semi-hardy foliage begonias like those in the Garden Angel series are bred to survive winter in a very sheltered spot.

Petunias have seen an explosion of breeding work resulting in some new and extraordinary hybrids, as here, with *Petunia* 'Night Sky'.

Embrace the trendy

Never is there a shortage of brand-spanking-new varieties to spark creative ideas for bedding displays, and these new hybrids and selections may be just the inspiration you need, the catalyst that takes you off on a completely different tangent and introduces you to flowers you'd never thought of trying before. Research and development to improve on existing varieties of floriferous plants is constant, and the stream of utterly new forms produced by hybridizers is nonstop as well. From extraordinary new colour breaks, novelty and stockier dwarf varieties, better weather-, pest-, and disease-resistant strains, and bigger and more boldly shaped blooms, to plants that flower for longer periods and highly unusual cultivars with extraordinary colour markings—all these are adding new options to the already wonderful existing range.

We now have yellow pelargoniums; petunias in almost every colour imaginable from pure white to jet black; bright-eyed osteospermums in both strong and subtle palettes; blousy, nearly fluorescent novelty begonias the size of dinner plates and complete with cancan skirts; stocky, self-supporting and freely branching dahlias with dark bronze-black foliage perfect for containers; semi-hardy foliage begonias in metallic textures; and blooms with extraordinarily striking and contrasting rims, dots, and stripes. Scent is also being bred back into all sorts of bedding flowers. Even beyond-boring wax begonias have been supercharged and re-engineered for a new millennium, turned into whoppingly wonderful flowering hulks that totally redefine this ultra-reliable but much-maligned plant. All these new trends in breeding and the resulting varieties are rather gloriously exciting.

PERENNIALS

As well as the traditional plants that come to mind for bedding out, there are always refreshingly new trends and plants that mean the world of flower-powered displays is constantly evolving. One such trend is that the range of plants we are bedding out increasingly includes hardy and half-hardy perennials. In particular, lots of herbaceous and shrubby first-year-flowering perennials

An increasing trend is the use of hardy and semi-hardy perennials, like these echinaceas, in floriferous temporary displays.

are growing in popularity. These can often be sown very early from seed or propagated from cuttings and will reach mature flowering size in just a few months. Plants like echinaceas, salvias, erysimums, and many others now feel like they belong just as much to the world of instant displays as traditional petunias and begonias.

DESIGNER PLANT COMBINATIONS

Offering ready-made plant combos is a big trend in garden centres. Compatibles, Seedsations, Kwik Kombos, One Touch, Custom Combos—all are similar ideas, co-ordinated designer plant combinations from different companies aimed to make things simple and straightforward for consumers and beginner gardeners.

Trixi series is a designer plant combination where three well-matched varieties of different species are grown together in the same plug. 'Trixi Cherry Kiss' features a deep magenta petunia, a pale candy pink calibrachoa, and a trailing cherry pink verbena.

Plants are sold in designer or garden packs or already growing together in a container. Whether different varieties of the same plant or completely different species, the plants grouped for sale in this way have a similar vigour and growth rate, enjoy the same climate conditions, or belong to a particular colour theme; sometimes, they are a selection of plants tolerant of a challenging garden situation, such as heat or shade. With all these options available, the results can be very successful.

Designer plugs usually contain three seeds which have been sown close together; these are often sold as a large jumbo plug or in a one-litre (one-quart) pot. Sometimes the trio offers varieties of the same plant in different colours, sometimes, a mix of plants. In any case, the idea is the same, that the three plants will look well together and develop in close harmony. Designer plugs work particularly well in hanging baskets, but, as with a modern meadow or annual seed mixture, the right combination is crucial for a beautifully balanced effect.

All designer plant combinations aim to take some of the guesswork out of gardening and are a great help to those of us short of inspiration or time. As a way of encouraging and helping people to grow plants well the first time around, and then to build on that experience and gain confidence, they're a great gateway into gardening.

CUTTING RAISED VS. SEED RAISED

I find that the most vigorous, outstanding plant varieties are the ones raised vegetatively from cuttings, often from sterile hybrids. They are often varieties that have been specially developed to be more pest- and disease-tolerant or repeat- or longer-flowering; many are polyploids, so have larger blooms or leaves; and, being sterile, they don't produce seed. The resulting plants are clones and are sometimes micropropagated, so that any virus or disease isn't passed on to young plants. They are uniform, often extremely robust, and reliable in terms of their garden performance.

Seed-raised plants are a great option for any keen gardener who has the time and facilities and who wants to raise large amounts of plants. Plants raised from open-pollinated seed are not as vigorous and can be variable, but they are generally much cheaper to produce, as the seed tends to be inexpensive.

F1 hybrids are produced by the careful and controlled crossing of two parent plants. Seed is more expensive but a better bet if you require very uniform and free-flowering plants. F1 hybrids can be the happy, dependable, and affordable medium between more costly, robust cutting-raised varieties and the most inexpensive mass-produced plants from open-pollinated stock. The increasing availability of F1 hybrid seed is a trend we can all embrace.

Cutting-raised trailing lobelias in the Waterfall series are an impressive example of much improved and much more robust plants.

VERTICAL BEDDING

Bedding plants can be used to great effect in vertical plantings, which, if it needs saying, are very on-trend. Choosing the most appropriate varieties and carefully considering all the environmental demands on the plants is critical, and with bedding that blooms nonstop, regular access for some deadheading and picking over is important, too. Some plants actually work best in vertical walls, planting pouches, Woolly Pockets, and planting towers; trailing and ivy leaf pelargoniums, foliage ipomoeas, calibrachoas, begonias, and drought-tolerant silver-leaved plants like jacobaeas and dichondras are some that come to mind. All are plants that are particularly good at coping with short periods of drought and stress from heat and also look great viewed from below and from the side. In vertical displays it is sometimes better to stick to the same types of plant and use all sorts of different-coloured cultivars together to create some eye-poppingly brilliant abstract effects. It's vertical "carpet bedding," and for me, big bold shapes and iconic graphic patterns work best. It's an investment to get a suitable system in place, and getting the irrigation and nutrition right is important, but once established and regularly picked over to keep plants in tip-top condition, a vertical display can present a truly stunning appearance.

This impressive black, silver, and white vertical display features *Ipomoea batatas* 'Suntory Black Tone', *Calibrachoa* 'Can-can Black Cherry', *Jacobaea maritima* 'Cirrus', *Dichondra argentea* 'Silver Falls', and *Lobelia erinus* 'Waterfall White Sparkle'.

plant care & cultivation

When it comes to deciding whether to grow our own plants for our seasonal displays or to buy, we're now in the most luxurious position. The options are almost endless. The range of plants offered—as seed or germinated seedlings, as mini, medium, postable, or jumbo plugs, as rooted cuttings or established trays, packs, and pots of ready-to-rock blooming beauties—is bigger than ever. The more time and growing facilities you have, the more of these options you can utilise and the more money you can save.

More and more the trend is to buy garden-ready pots that simply need planting and watering in; with an occasional liquid feed, they will grow and bloom all season long. It couldn't be more simple. However, it really is so much fun and incredibly rewarding and satifying to grow a few of the plants you'll be caring for yourself, from seed, cuttings, or plugs, and to propagate them by layering or division. If you can find the time and space, have a go. You'll be surprised just how easy it is.

Growing from seed

I find raising my own plants from seed hugely rewarding. I pick really easy plants like sunflowers, nasturtiums, and cosmos, and even with just a few pots and trays on warm bright indoor window ledges, I get good results. Some seed is a little more tricky to germinate. Sowing lots of seed and then pricking out, potting on, and hardening off requires time, committment, and a fair amount of frost-free growing space. You need a certain amount of skill and, ideally, a greenhouse. Often seed is sold as a mixture, a range of different colours, and so growing just the particular variety you want isn't always straightforward. You might be surprised at both the cost and sometimes the meagre amount of seed enclosed in a packet. So if you require only a few plants of a specific variety, then—weighing up the costs of all the

equipment, the risks, and the time—buying a few plugs or plants can be a much better bet.

However, if you do have some room and can find the funds for even just a propagator or heated mat to kick things off, then I would encourage you wholeheartedly to give growing your own a go. What money can't buy is the joy and satisfaction of raising your own plants from seed. The pleasure your homegrown plants will give you as they bloom all summer long is deeply rewarding, especially when they inspire a natter and mutual moment of adoration with a neighbour. The seed companies also seem to be slowly realising that rather than just multicoloured mixes (great as they are for a "flowers gone mad in a sweet shop" feel), modern gardeners want specific, single-colour varieties. So as ever in the world of bedding out, things are moving forward and evolving.

DIRECT SOWING

Many hardy annuals and biennials are easiest and do best sown direct outdoors, either in early spring or in the summer and autumn the year before you want them to flower. Classic examples include pot marigolds, California poppies, and hollyhocks. Many form a type of taproot system that hates to be disturbed or transplanted, and so sowing direct is not only quick, easy, and far less fussy than individual pots, it yields far better results. Choose a level, thoroughly weeded and finely raked-over bit of ground for them in a bright spot. You can use sand to clearly mark out the specific areas where you have sown different varieties. Sprinkle the seed thinly, and very gently rake it into the soil surface; and water lightly, too. To stop birds from disturbing the seed, I usually cover the ground with horticultural fleece just for the first few weeks. It's that easy. A more modern method is to mix up all your different hardy annuals to make a sort of colourful meadow mix and sprinkle it liberally over an area you've prepared in the same way in early spring. If you have lots of different types of plants that flower at different times, you should get a staggered flowering period that lasts for months. This is how a lot of traditional hardy annual flower seed is packaged and sold, as colour-themed mixes, and I'm all for them.

A LITTLE BOTTOM HEAT

Some of the most gloriously floriferous half-hardy and tender plants will need constant gentle bottom heat for good germination. For ageratums, begonias, dahlias, lobelias, French marigolds, nemesias, verbenas, zinnias, and other much-loved favourites, 18–21°C (65–70°F) is good. Others (e.g., impatiens, pelargoniums, petunias, salvias) like it warmer, at a toasty 24°C (75°F). Heated mats and propagators are a great investment if you really are going all out to grow lots from seed, and some are designed to fit perfectly in window bottoms. Not having a greenhouse doesn't have to stop you having a go. If you have a bright window bottom that's above a radiator, then this can work well, too. If you sow seeds in small containers and enclose them in a plastic bag with a few holes for ventilation, then you have a good warm propagation environment. If you don't have a greenhouse, sow slightly later, towards the end of the recommended sowing period. Ideally, once plants are ready for pricking out or potting on, you'll be close to the time when frosts have finished, if you're mainly going to grow on young plants in a sheltered outdoor spot.

Half-hardy and tender plants are fun and exciting to have a go at from seed. The success of growing dahlias, coleus, or pelargoniums (these three aren't too tricky) is really quite addictive. Constant warmth, light, and moist (but not wet) conditions are key.

MODULAR TRAYS

Modular trays make things quick and easy. I now sow almost all my seeds into different-sized modular trays. I'm often really time-poor just as the gardening season goes into fifth gear in spring. When I finally find the time to prick things out, I'm usually a few weeks too late, and seedlings can be overcrowded and difficult to divide and pull apart without harming the roots. But using modular trays means I've almost eliminated the need for pricking out altogether, as each plant is already spaced and has its own mini–growing module.

SEED COMPOST

Always invest in fresh top-quality seed compost when growing bedding plants from scratch. Think of it like flour for baking bread and cakes. You want high quality, you want it as fresh as possible, and you want just enough for your bake. Choose specialist seed compost, not multipurpose compost, particularly for the types of bedding plants that need warmth and cosseting to start. It's worth asking if it's new stock, as compost that has been sitting around outside—exposed to wet, cold weather for months—is not a great investment. I buy small-sized bags of seed compost, and I prefer traditional John Innes loam-based types. Use the whole bag in one go, if possible, or buy a resealable bag.

The range of available composts can be daunting. The best material for young plants is a good-quality compost for seed or cuttings; buy a small (or at least resealable) bag.

Homemade compost is far from suitable for sowing seeds; it's full of fungal spores, bacteria, and all sorts of useful microorganisms that are great for mature and established plants, but the seedlings of most bedding plants will struggle to compete in such a biologically active home brew. Use homemade compost as a mulch or soil improver in beds and borders and under trees and shrubs.

KEEP IT CLEAN

Giving your seeds the best start possible means keeping everything—tools, seed trays, modules, plug trays, and pots—fresh and super-clean. Carefully wash any pots and equipment you're reusing in hot soapy water first. Wash away debris and fungal spores and make things as spick and span as possible. Remember to make sure your watering can and misters are clean, too. Your seedlings are precious and vulnerable things, and damping off or grey mould (botrytis) can quickly take hold and kill the lot.

LIGHT REQUIREMENTS

Always check light requirements before sowing. Don't make the mistake of covering fine seed that requires good light for germination with compost. Snapdragons, begonias, coleus, gaillardias, gerberas, nicotianas, petunias, and most primulas are just a few of the plants that prefer light for germination. Seed should be sprayed lightly with a fine mist and kept gently warm and moist and left on the surface. Cover over the works with something clear that lets light in—and keeps in humidity and warmth. Make sure moisture doesn't build up too much, however, and make things too wet. Ventilation is important. Once the majority of seedlings have shot up, cool things down and ventilate well; and after a day or two, remove the cover and put the youngsters somewhere bright but out of strong direct sunlight.

For types of seed that can be covered, use vermiculite rather than compost, as its structure is light and airy (so seedlings can push up through it), and it's completely sterile, too. It can also absorb and retain moisture, releasing it slowly as required and so preventing the seeds from sitting in too much water. In addition, the air

pockets in its structure insulate and protect the seeds from potentially damaging temperature extremes. A formulation of vermiculite and perlite is sometimes sold as a "seed blanket."

The seeds of calendulas, gazanias, and nemesias prefer darkness to germinate and should be covered with a layer of fine-sieved seed compost; however, these are the exceptions to the rule.

Most commercially produced seed is bred and selected for its ease of germination, so your chances of success are high—if you carefully follow the instructions and tips on the packet.

WATERING AND PRICKING OUT

Go easy when watering seedlings. Too much wet can cause roots and stems to rot. Be sparing, and use a very gentle fine rose or, even better, a pump-action mister. Don't use water that's been sitting and stagnating in a water butt. Your seedlings are too vulnerable to expose them to a soup of microorganisms. Use clean, fresh water.

Prick out seedlings very gently and remember the golden rule: hold them by a true leaf, never by their stem. Stems bruise easily.

Always hold young plants and seedlings by a true leaf when pricking out.

Enjoy trying something new from seed each year. Share or swap half-packets or excess seedlings and plants with friends, neighbours, and family. Setting up or joining a local gardening group on a social networking site is a great way of offering plants for swapping, asking for advice, and posting pictures of your challenges and triumphs.

Growing from softwood cuttings

Extra plants can be raised from cuttings by looking for nonflowering shoots and stem tips in the spring and summer months on all sorts of bedding plants. For some classic groups such as pelargoniums and fuchsias, cuttings are traditionally taken in late summer to make a crop of new young plants for the following year. However, throughout the growing season, shoot tips and stems that you remove or shorten to encourage a plant to branch and bush out can sometimes be perfect material for cuttings.

Collect material in the early morning, ideally, when it's turgid and full of water. If there are a few flower buds present, remove them. Cut off all the leaves from the lower half of the shoot and make a clean straight cut underneath the lowest leaf joint. Fill a small terracotta pot with free-draining sandy compost. Dip the bottom of cuttings into organic rooting powder and, after inserting a dibber or pencil to make holes that are the depth of half the length of the cutting, place them in the compost around the edge of the pot. Water in very gently and then cover the pot with a disposable clear shower cap (the kind you get free in hotels) or a clear plastic bag. Snip a couple of holes into the cover for ventilation and make sure it's supported by a couple of short canes and not touching the leaves of the cuttings. Keep the cuttings in a brightly lit place (but not in direct sun) and, if possible, on a warm heated mat or in a propagator.

I am regularly surprised at just how quick and easy it is to propagate all sorts of plants in this way. It's such a simple method and I think always worth a try with any young fresh growing material.

I have a bright sunny kitchen window bottom that is quickly filled up with cuttings and young plants in spring.

I use disposable shower caps I collect from hotel stays to make mini-propagators for cuttings and seeds.

Growing from semi-ripe cuttings

Semi-ripe cuttings are usually taken slightly later in the growing season, from summer until mid autumn. The base material of a semi-ripe cutting should be starting to mature and feel slightly stiff and woody, whereas the tip is still quite young and soft. Sometimes it's beneficial to have a tiny "heel" of material where the cutting is pulled away with a piece of the mature stem. Trim excess leaves and pot up in the same way as for softwood cuttings.

Growing from basal cuttings

These are very similar to softwood and semi-ripe cuttings, except they are usually taken from clusters of fresh young shoots at the base or crown of herbaceous plants in spring. Dahlias, echinaceas, delphiniums, gaillardias, lupins, and salvias are often propagated this way. Pick sturdy shoots, 5–7 cm (2–2.75 in.) in length. Use a very sharp knife and remove shoots as close to the base as possible, with a tiny part of the woody basal tissue attached. Then treat exactly as you would a softwood cutting.

Growing from root cuttings

Root cuttings are best taken in mid to late autumn, when plants are entering a dormant period. A range of herbaceous plants can be propagated using this method, including eryngiums and phlox. Select a few young, vigorous thick roots and cut them off close to the crown of the plant. Cut sections around 5 cm (2 in.) in length and then plant them horizontally in a gritty compost about 2 cm (0.8 in.) deep. Keep frost-free, and the root cutting will develop shoots and a new root system over the next six months.

Growing from plugs

I buy more and more plug plants these days. The most difficult job of germination or micropropagation (taking a tiny cutting) has already been done, and the plant is already on its way to forming a robust root system and gearing itself up for the growing season ahead. Young plug plants are inexpensive, and you can buy small amounts, often just an individual specimen of exactly the variety or colour you need.

The increasing range of plug plants on offer, and often sold individually, makes it so easy to grow a huge range of different plants, resulting in much more diverse and varied displays. They're brilliant for container gardeners and those of us with small suburban gardens that don't need an ocean of lobelias or begonias.

Plug plants galore.

Plugs are such an inexpensive treat, who could blame you for snapping them up and saving yourself a lot of work? If you plan your display well in advance and carefully calculate exactly how many plants you really need, then buying plugs rather than garden-ready plants can save you a lot of money, and it doesn't really cost that much more than growing them yourself. Here are some tips for growing plug plants.

KEEP PLUGS SLIGHTLY MOIST AT ALL TIMES

Whether you order your plants online and they arrive through the post or you buy them at the garden centre or nursery, be sure to take them out of their packaging straight away and soak them in water until they are thoroughly wetted. If you can't pot them up right away, drain them off and keep them somewhere airy, light, and on the slightly cool side, but out of direct sun and away from drying winds. The sooner you can pot them up, the better.

Keep baby plugs moist, and pot them up immediately.

LARGER PLUGS CAN BE A BETTER BET

Plug plants come in lots of different sizes, and often at the larger garden centres you can get bargain offers and "pick and mix" deals that allow you to buy a wide range of plants you need just a small number of. In early spring the very smallest mini-plugs need longer to grow on and must be cared for in a bright, frost-free but relatively cool place, before final hardening off and planting out. My advice is don't buy too many too early, especially if the long-term weather forecast means you'll be molly-coddling baby plants for weeks. Wait until the weather's a little more promising and go for medium and jumbo plugs later in the season, particularly if space is an issue.

POT ON, PINCH OUT, AND TAKE CHEEKY CUTTINGS

Often the larger-sized plugs can be planted straight into containers, planting pouches, and baskets, but they still need to be hardened off. I think it's often easier and better to pot them up into a smallish pot (say, 7–9 cm, 2.75–3.5 in.), pinch out tips, and grow them on slightly first to make a good strong plant.

As plug plants grow, they need trimming or pinching out to encourage bushy growth. You can often snip some shoots just underneath a leaf node and use these quite small bits of plant material as cuttings. You might think they're too small and won't root, but often young plant material near the tips and leaf axils is full of plant

growth regulators (hormones)—given the right conditions, such material will root in no time at all. I've often obtained extra plants from plugs of fuchsias, felicias, begonias, argyranthemums, dianthus, dahlias, coleus, lantanas, iresines, ipomoeas, pelargoniums, verbenas, torenias, scaevolas, plectranthus, osteospermums—the list increases as I get more thrifty and adventurous. If you're in doubt, just have a snip and dip. You've got nothing to lose.

Division

Dividing up a mature clump or mat of a perennial plant is one of the very easiest ways to get more plants for free. You can often be quite brutal and chop these types of plants apart and get great results. Most perennials (e.g., agapanthus, ajugas, dahlias, euphorbias, primulas, salvias, zantedeschias) benefit from division every few years in any case, to maintain their vigour and vitality. Division is usually best performed just as the plants are about to start into active growth in early spring. The key with most perennials is making sure the clump or mat is cut up fairly into sections that all have young growth and evidence of new young shoots attached. Dig up or knock out plants from their pot and really observe the crown or growing point for new young shoots. You can literally cut up the clump with an old bread knife or spade and then pot on into good compost and water. Coax them into growth gently in a warm, sheltered spot.

Layering

Layered shoots form roots while they're still attached to the parent plant. Many spreading and sprawling plants will naturally self-layer, as their shoots touch the soil surface, whether in containers or when growing as a groundcover. To encourage this, use paper clips to pin stems down and keep the soil surface moist by spraying daily with water. Many of the trailing foliage plants used in bedding displays (e.g., dichondras, plectranthus) are easily propagated in this way.

Keep things cool

Growing young bedding plants on in cool (but not cold) and well-ventilated conditions encourages sturdy, stocky growth. If young plants experience too much warmth for too long, it leads to weak and leggy plants that never fully recover in terms of their shape and stature. Once seeds have germinated and cuttings have rooted, it's really best to try to take temperatures down to around 15°C (60°F) and keep light levels as constant as you can. Easy enough if you have a greenhouse and can make a small warm section for propagation and have the rest of the house as a cooler space for growing on. However, if you're making do with just a propagator or warm sunny windowsills, it's all about timing the growing of your plants. When they have rooted and are really starting to grow away, it should be (fingers crossed) far enough into the growing season to put them in a sheltered spot outdoors in the daytime to grow. So don't sow seed or take cuttings too early in the season, if you're limited for growing space. Wait until spring is well underway.

Buying tips

More and more we are buying garden-ready plants. Be choosy and shop around for the best price. Ideally, buy quality, and support good growers: some local growers, independent garden centres, and nurseries grow much of their stock themselves. Enquire if they do and how they do it. If they are also doing their bit to cultivate their plants along more organic lines by using fewer sprays and chemicals, then in my opinion that's well worth encouraging.

Timing and price tend to be linked. A garden-ready plant in summer may seem expensive, but all the work has been done for you, and it's grown to perfection and ready to bloom all season long. A month or two earlier, you could probably have bought a pack of four or six of the exact same plant for less. So if you're on a budget, try to buy earlier. For the best selection and amazing range of plants for bedding out, go online in winter and early spring and explore the websites of the seed, plug, and young plant companies. There are often good offers to be had if you order well in advance of planting season, and sometimes you get free postage and packing deals for large orders, too.

Plant qualities to look for are fresh, perky green leaves, a bushy compact habit, and strong stems with lots of buds. It can be worth very gently knocking a plant out from its pot to check that its roots are healthy and have filled the pot but aren't spiralling or overly congested. Avoid plants that are totally potbound or shedding leaves, or that have any signs of damaged stems, discoloured or yellowing foliage, or obvious signs of pests or disease. Any that have already been flowering for a good while and have lots of deadheads and fallen flowers should be left on the bench, as should any that look stressed from being allowed to completely dry out or are sopping wet and thoroughly waterlogged.

Always acclimatise or harden off plants when you get them home by putting them in a sheltered spot outside in the day and bringing them in at night. In spring, make sure frosts have finished before permanently planting out—and have some horticultural fleece to hand, just in case.

Buy a few of a diverse range of types but be realistic about numbers. You often need fewer plants than you think to create an amazing display. On the whole, bedding plants grow quickly and if they're happy, they'll soon bulk out and fill gaps.

A well-stocked garden centre can be a fun place to buy plants. Ask how they are grown, and make sure specimens are in top-notch condition.

BLOOMING ORGANIC

If you're a committed organic gardener, sourcing organically grown bedding plants can be a challenge. Generally speaking, bedding plant production is an intense and inorganic process; on the other hand, many growers are moving towards using totally peat-free and recycled growing media, and production is often specialised, precision- and computer-controlled, and therefore highly energy-efficient.

The short amount of time between sowing and selling leaves little room for mistakes. Plant pests and diseases can't be allowed to drastically reduce quantity or quality. The prevention of any diseases or damage to young seedling plants is key; and in general, problems in production are usually attributable to diseases like damping off and grey mould, so fungicidal drenches are often applied to growing media. The commercial cultivation process relies on high levels of sanitation and the presence of systemic pesticides in growing media, often types of neonicotinoids, to control aphids, whiteflies, vine weevils, sciarid flies, and other potential problem pests. These chemicals help to protect seedlings and young plants from attack from pathogens as they develop and grow, and in general are used in a very targeted manner and in closed, carefully monitored glasshouse environments. However, it is fair to say that there are concerns, chief among them that certain neonicotinoids could be linked to declines in bees and other pollinators. Their persistence in the soil and in the pollen and nectar of blooms (and hence their potential toxicity to bees) has been the subject of recent scientific studies. Research into the full effects of neonicotinoids in the complex situation of pollinator decline is ongoing, but some nurseries have taken steps to source only plants grown without these chemicals, which is a positive step forward for all our pollinators.

The availability of organically grown bedding and ornamental plants will increase when demand for them increases from gardeners like us. I believe that growing and gardening in an environmentally friendly way is simply the right thing to do. I also think as gardeners we need to ask questions and make requests, and let our local garden centres, growers, and nurseries know that along with organic vegetable plants, we want organic bedding plants, too, and that we will support and buy them if they stock them.

For now, however, growing your own plants from seed—using natural, sustainable, and organically approved materials—is your best option to be blooming organic.

Hardening off

Most bedding plants need to be prepared for life out-side. Whether they are plants from the garden centre or homegrown, most will need a careful introduction to outdoor conditions. Summer bedding certainly can't be put outside until all threat of frosts has passed and plants can be protected from a few chilly nights. As soon as you dare, start placing plants outside during the day in a sheltered spot or cold frame to get some fresh air and wind movement to encourage robust, stocky growth. Bring them indoors or undercover at night, or cover with fleece. Don't leave tender plants outside if temperatures are predicted to fall below 5°C (41°F).

I like to get my seedlings and young plants outside as much as possible on warm spring days. Every window ledge and patio bench is fully utilised!

Soils and compost

On the whole, most full-on floriferous seasonal plants require a fertile soil or compost to grow in. Don't believe old tales about these plants loving very poor, thin soils, as in the vast majority of cases, it's just not true. Good drainage is essential, along with readily available nutri-ents and a good amount of organic matter. If planting into existing beds and borders in your garden, it's well worth thoroughly weeding and then slightly enriching these areas first. Ideally, use pelleted or very well rotted manure, which shouldn't smell. The next best thing to use is your own garden compost or leaf mould. Lightly fork over into the top 10 cm (4 in.) of the soil surface.

When it comes to containers, it's even more important to get a really good mixture for your plants to grow in. These smaller restricted volumes of growing media have to work much harder to provide everything your plants need throughout the growing season. I tend not to choose the usual peat, coir, or recycled-bark multipur-pose types that are available commercially. I prefer to use loam-based composts as my base material. They are usually that bit heavier, so great stability-wise, and much easier to rewet when containers dry out. There are lots of peat-reduced and peat-free multipurpose composts available, often stacked high and on offer. I find them disappointing in terms of their structure and organic content. If you're on a tight budget, however, use the big bale types of cheap-as-chips compost as your base material. Enrich them as you use them. They need fleshing out, so add handfuls of well-rotted manure, a half cup of poultry manure pellets or slow-release fertiliser, and some leaf mould and garden compost, if you can get hold of some. Ash from a wood-burning stove is great for a hit of extra potash (i.e., potassium), and charcoal can help prevent a compost mixture from becoming stagnant and sour, so sprinkle a handful into your mix with some vermiculite, grit, or sand to further open it up.

I like to keep things as natural as possible, so I pre-fer to use concentrated organic seaweed and liquid comfrey-based tomato-type (i.e., high in potassium) feeds across the growing season. These always work well for my displays.

Planting out

Once frosts are a thing of the past and plants have been acclimatised or hardened off for at least a week, it's safe to plant outdoors. Be cautious, though. Half-hardy and tender summer-flowering plants will sit, sulk, and look like they're refusing to grow in very cool, wet weather. You may be keen for summer to get in its swing, but hold off planting out until the long-range forecast is good. When planting out bedding, my granddad would pinch out any flowers in full bloom. He did this to encourage the plants to get their roots down and to concentrate on growing and establishing themselves first. He would also snip the roots of any plants that were a little potbound or congested in their pots. By giving a plant a short respite from flowering and breaking a few bound-up roots, you can help kick-start the production of new feeding roots and fresh growth and get growth off to a flying start. It may seem cruel to remove blooms and cut a root or two, but it can pay dividends if you want well-established plants that will bloom even longer over a really long season.

Hanging baskets

If you're a flower fanatic like me, and more than partial to the odd petunia, then your hanging baskets are your badge of honour. Where I grew up, you were judged by the quality and the floriferousness of them and your standard fuchsias. If your baskets couldn't perform all summer long—well, you and your lot weren't up to much.

Hanging baskets can get a bad press from snobby horticultural types, but they are incredibly useful for bringing colour and interest to hard-to-reach spots. Summer baskets are best planted up in early spring and then grown on under glass, so they have time to establish and fill out before going outside. For really impressive baskets, I've learnt a few things over the years. Here are some top tips for happy hanging.

THE BASKET

Don't bother with really small baskets—with very small, invariably shallow hanging baskets, you're on a hiding to nothing. They contain very little compost, and they dry out quickly. They will run you ragged as you try to keep them from total desiccation. Go as big as you can. Obviously, make sure the supports you have in place to hold them are sufficiently strong and properly fixed. Check the works at the beginning of every season. If you're as hopeless as I am at DIY, then get a professional to put hooks and brackets up for you.

Choose "closed" basket types for very hot, sunny gardens; in such gardens, closed baskets with generous in-built or clip-on drip trays can be a huge benefit. After watering, the basket will quickly absorb any extra water at the bottom, and it encourages the roots to grow down towards the base of the basket. Often these types of baskets don't need a liner either.

Other than that, the style and type of basket is yours to choose. You can turn pretty much any container into a hanging basket. Just drill a few drainage holes and some others for hooks or wires, and you're off and running. It's all down to your personal preference—and whatever your choice, it's really not that important after the first few weeks. If your hanging basket is planted properly, the trailing plants will often completely cover and disguise it anyway. What's more important is how well your basket is planted and its ability to retain some moisture.

THE LINER

My preferred lining for virtually all baskets or hanging containers is a preformed coir or jute type. Not only do these have a natural-looking finish, which helps if they can be seen through the sides of a traditional wire basket, but they are easy to cut to shape if necessary and often reusable too, so—great value. The majority of baskets will also need some sort of reservoir at the base that allows the basket to retain a small amount of water after each watering. Simply cut out a circle from the side of a polythene bag of compost, and place this in the bottom of the basket; this should allow for a shallow saucer-like area that will retain water only in the bottom

3 cm (1.2 in.) of compost. Any deeper, and it could be more of a hindrance than a help, causing waterlogging.

My top tip is this—don't cut holes or slits into the side of your liner. This is contrary to the traditional advice to plant up the sides, cutting holes in the liner and inserting trailing plants as you fill up the basket with compost. I prefer to position trailing plants around the rim of the basket to sprawl over the edge. Hanging baskets lose water so easily, and cutting holes into the side of the liner means that water and nutrients will run through that much faster. In a hot, windy summer, this will make watering that much more of a challenge.

THE COMPOST

For baskets, use fresh top-quality compost every time. There are types specially formulated for summer baskets which already contain controlled- and slow-release fertilisers and water-retaining granules. They are slightly more expensive but cut out the guesswork. If you're using a plain multipurpose compost, mix in a slow- or controlled-release fertiliser and water-retaining granules for best results.

THE PLANTS

When it comes to the number of plants to place in a basket, it's hard not to go over the top. But that's exactly what you want most of them to do: grow vigorously and trail over the brim and down the sides of the basket. It's traditional to have a main short plant in the centre, one with an upright habit, and a group of three plants with mounding or bushy habits around it to give the middle of the basket some height and oomph. Most baskets are viewed from below, so your trailers and sprawlers, usually five or six planted towards the edge, are the ones most likely to steal the show. I tend to go for a looser mix of fillers and spillers. I think a combination of trailing and mounding plants feels more relaxed. Be sure to give each plant room to grow and intermingle. As a very rough guide—in a basket that is 30 cm (12 in.) in diameter, seven to nine plants is plenty.

This large Strawberries and Cream–themed basket contains just nine plants, and by early summer its black plastic container is nearly hidden.

AFTERCARE

Ideally, your hanging baskets will have been grown under glass for the first few weeks. It's easy to overwater at this stage, so go carefully. Water them sparingly at first. Plugs and young plants won't like sitting in a big volume of sopping-wet compost. Once growing well and in their final positions, however, baskets will need more regular watering and a weekly liquid feed of a high-potassium fertiliser to encourage blooms. The slow- or controlled-release feed in the compost will not sustain the plants into late summer. Depending on their particular location, at the height of summer, many baskets will need watering every other day or even every day; it's best to do this early in the morning or as the sun sets in the evening. The "up-down" type pulleys, especially the spring-loaded ones, are great for watering, feeding, and avoiding any falls from wobbly step ladders; they also help hugely when it comes to picking over. A lance with a fitted fertiliser applicator that fits on your existing hose is also a great investment if you don't have pulley systems in place.

Watering and feeding

The amount of feed and water that bedding plants require to bloom and perform at their very best is affected by lots of different factors. Smaller pots and hanging baskets in hot, sunny, exposed spots will often dry out in no time and need watering every day. Plants in large containers in sheltered semi-shady locations may only need a thorough watering twice a week. In general, however, most plants that have been bedded out need a thorough regular watering and feeding every few days throughout the summer and even more so in dry, sunny spells.

It's tempting to keep things simple and go around and give everything a total soaking, whether needed or not. However, the compost that your plants are growing in can quickly become waterlogged, exhausted, and rather washed out. The idea is that you want to water as little as possible but, when you do, as thoroughly as you

can. It's a good thing to let containers dry out just slightly between waterings to encourage roots to head down deep for moisture. This promotes strong, resilient plants.

Feed and water either in the evening as the sun is fading or in early morning, well before things heat up. Make sure pots have drip trays, so they have the opportunity to soak up moisture that drains straight through. Don't leave pots standing in water for longer than a few hours afterwards. Heavily waterlogged soil conditions are often more deadly to bedding plants than a short drought.

When bedded out in borders, growing in good garden soil, plants often need extra encouragement only later in midsummer from a good organic liquid feed once a week. This will supply an extra boost of potassium and phosphate, which helps to promote the formation of flower buds and keeps plants blooming well into late summer. Yellowing leaves, few flowers, or poor growth are signs that you may need to give your plants more regular liquid feeds.

Plants in containers need a more regular feeding regime and can quickly exhaust the nutrients that were initially present in their compost. I use organic slow-release fertilisers. They can take time to degrade and release nutrients but are helped along by soil microorgan-isms, which are in turn influenced by soil temperature. Hoof-and-horn and bone meal are both effective but should be applied really early in the growing season, so that there's plenty of time for them to break down and get to work.

Controlled-release fertilisers are most often granules of inorganic chemicals. They are usually coated with a porous material. Water enters, and the fertiliser seeps out into the surrounding compost. They are designed to respond quickly to increasing temperatures, releas-ing more fertiliser in warm soils, which corresponds to faster plant growth and development in favourable weather. The thickness of the coating that surrounds the granules is variable, either increasing or restricting the leaching rate of fertiliser, so they can be designed to feed plants for different growth periods. The blooming performance of hanging baskets which utilise these controlled-release fertilisers is extraordinarily impressive.

I am evangelical, however, about organic concentrated feeds containing seaweed extract. Seaweed can be rich in trace elements. Plants need only tiny amounts of these nutrients, but common fertilisers often lack them, and they can be depleted in soils that are heavily irrigated on a regular basis. There are lots of dried and processed seaweed feeds available. I like the ones that are applied as foliar feeds, where the nutrients are sprayed onto the foliage and can be taken up quickly into the sap through the leaves. They can be great in a "cure-all" way, helping struggling plants to get through periods of lacklustre growth. They can also help to revitalise a group of plants that has suffered an infestation of a particular pest or disease.

Young plants that have yet to reach maturity and need to bush out, grow on, and produce more leaves, stems, and shoots will need a balanced feed, with plenty of nitrogen. Look for the NPK ratio on the packet. The number for N (nitrogen) should be slightly higher than the numbers for P (phosphorus) and K (potassium).

Plants that have reached maturity and mainly need support to either kick-start blooming or to maintain their floriferousness into late summer will need a balanced feed that delivers increased levels of phosphorus and potassium. If your plants are all leaf and no flower, however, use some sulphate of potash; it's a fast-acting fertiliser to quickly boost flowering and ripening of fruit. Otherwise, several readily available fertiliser options have formulations perfect for prolonging flowering.

To save some money, grow a big patch of Russian comfrey (*Symphytum ×uplandicum*) and make your own concentrated liquid feed. Two or three times a year, you can cut the comfrey to the ground, chop up all the stems and leaves, and then steep them in water to make an evil-smelling but very effective plant feed and tonic that promotes flowering. The same can be done with stinging nettle (*Urtica dioica*), which makes a nitrogen-rich feed best used early in the growing season. Try to leave some nettles year-round for the butterflies to lay eggs on, however.

For the most floriferous displays in containers and hanging baskets, I find a combination of slow- or controlled-release fertiliser topped up with regular but dilute organic liquid feeds that specifically encourage flowering is the magic recipe.

Mulching

I'm surprised how few gardeners mulch their summer containers and other bedding plant displays. This is an example of when mulching can have the most impact, particularly in a hot, dry summer and on light and sharply draining soils. I'm a big fan of different types of gravel and small pebbles, and I try to reuse them every year; however, there is now an incredible range of decorative mulches available, and I would encourage anyone to invest in them. Besides bringing extra interest to a display, they can add weight and stability, make weeding a thing of the past, and prevent "plant decapitation" and other hoeing accidents. Many bedding plants are quite shallow-rooting, so mulching can have a massive impact by cutting down on evaporation from the soil surface, meaning less watering and more time to sit back, relax, and enjoy your efforts. Organic mulches like well-rotted manure and leaf mould will break down and add organic matter to the soil, and Strulch (a mineralised mulch made from straw) has an added advantage: slugs and snails seem to hate travelling across it. Very dry or rough materials like fine sharp grit or wool pellets are also good for scattering over the soil surface, and they too deter slugs and snails.

Staking and supporting

The most commonly grown bedding plants are usually well-branched dwarf varieties that have strong central stems; they are stocky and short and require no staking at all. However, if you don't want to limit yourself to just short varieties, there are lots of taller, looser, informal-style plants from which to choose. I like to vary heights and habits in a display, and some of the best, bigger-blooming, lofty plants will need supports. So will lovely annual climbers. Grow these up wigwams of long willow and hazel twigs, which you can usually intertwine and make very decorative. I also love rusted metal frames, specially made for climbing plants, in pots and borders. They are expensive, but considering the years of use you will almost certainly get, they are not so pricey over the long haul. Growing ornamental climbing plants up green netting doesn't display them to their best; and besides, the netting is often a bit too flimsy. A strong gust could dismantle the lot. A trellis is a better bet, and if anchored well in the first place and prestained with a wood preservative, it will often last for years.

Ugly or obvious staking can spoil the whole display. Whatever your choice of supports, get them in place nice and early, and lots of plants will rest and take support from them as they grow up and through them, rather than being formally tied in. I've started to invest in lots of different green plastic-coated metal supports; the supports are usually totally disguised by foliage in a week or two, and it's easy to pull them up, or twist them to adjust their height. They're a great investment, too, as they're endlessly reusable and easily stacked and stored in a shed over winter.

Good old-fashioned green jute twine is possibly the best thing ever invented. My granddad used it, and I do too, usually at double thickness. Always loosely tie the plant to the stake or support. I hate to see any plant trussed up and overly tied in.

Pinching out, picking over, and deadheading

Pinching out the growing tips of lots of different types of plants, but especially trailing and spreading ones, encourages them to make sideshoots, grow in a more compact way, and produce more flowers. Picking over and removing any dead leaves and flowers also keeps your plants and displays looking really fresh.

The key is doing a little and often—ideally, as soon as you notice a plant or container needs attention. If you can find just five or ten minutes every day to spruce up your bedding out, it's often all that's required throughout the season. I have a pair of scissors by both the front and back door, and a plastic tub and a watering can with feed in it, always at the ready. I prefer to cut off deadheads, as hands soon get sticky and sappy from decaying petals. Also, flowers and petals can fall off, leaving behind the basal part of a bloom, which turns into a fruit or seedhead; it's best to snip the little pedicels or stalks of blooms to remove the whole thing.

I try to make all this a part of my daily routine and fit in a spontaneous "spruce up" just before I'm off out or as I arrive home. This way, I can get that never-ending quest for floral perfection out of my system, and then relax and get on with my day or evening. It's important not to let things go too far, as plants that haven't been deadheaded or picked over can quickly look scruffy. It can be hard to coax some plants back into full-on flower production if energy has been diverted into seed production; they lose their floral mojo and end up limping through the rest of the summer. Seed formation can initiate the production of certain plant growth regulators, and these hormones work to stop flower bud formation.

Some self-shedding varieties will drop their flowers naturally as they go over, and many F1 or sterile hybrids don't make seed, so these are a great choice if you really can't make time to pick over a display very often. For me, however, it's a welcome excuse to get out of the house and have a stress-busting screen-break moment and mingle with my blooms. It's one of my favourite gardening activities and allows me to indulge my slightly obsessive-compulsive tidying tendencies for just a short spell.

Overwintering

I try to keep many of the perennials I use in my displays from one year to the next. With all these key plants, it's worth a good rummage for milky white vine weevil grubs among the roots and crowns before storing. Remove them and feed them to the birds, as otherwise the grubs will happily eat your roots and tubers all through the winter. It's also a good idea to take off a lot of the soft sappy leafy material, particularly of the more tender tropical-type plants, before storing or moving.

I love to reuse borderline hardy perennial foliage plants like heucheras, tiarellas, unusual ivies, and certain grasses. These plants can be at risk if they're planted in small, poorly insulated containers, as the pot could freeze solid, causing severe damage or death to the root ball; so place them in a sheltered spot.

Tender plants that have tubers or thick fleshy storage roots—dahlias, cannas, foliage ipomoeas, and begonias, for example—are easy to dry off slightly and store in a dark frost-free place. For dahlias, you can wait right up until the frosts blacken the foliage, and then cut back; leave upside down for a few days, so moisture drains out of the hollow stems, and then store. Pretty much all others should be stored well before the first frosts arrive, however. They all do well in trays or boxes surrounded by sand or compost that is only the slightest bit moist and, ideally, loosely wrapped individually in newspaper-like parcels, so that they don't dry out too much. As long as they don't get too wet and rot, or totally dry out and desiccate, they will quietly rest in a cool (7–10°C, 45–50°F) dark environment. In spring, they can be gently coaxed into growth in pots of fresh compost in a greenhouse or on warm window bottoms indoors.

My bright south-facing kitchen and spare bedroom window bottoms have become sort of winter holding areas for a number of plants during the worst of the winter months. Here I help fuchsias, pelargoniums, coleus, and all sorts of succulents and foliage plants survive until spring. The key is keeping them in good light and on the dry side. Water very sparingly.

Pests and diseases

With so many different types of plants involved in a bedding display, the number of pests and diseases that could cause a problem is extensive. If your plants have been grown well, however, and are healthy and free of pests and diseases when you plant, then the list of things that are likely to cause problems is pretty small. Still, it's best to be prepared and proactive.

Plants that are struggling because they are undernourished, overwatered, allowed to dry out for too long, or planted in a badly drained soggy patch or in heavy shade—stressed, in other words—will invariably attract problem pests and never grow well. So first and foremost, be sure to get your location, soil, and preparation right. A happy, healthy plant will be better equipped to cope with any pest and disease problems from the off.

Prevention is always better than cure. If you're well equipped and have a few things to hand, you can deal with any issues quickly as soon as you notice them. Spotting and treating things early helps avert any major problems.

SLUGS AND SNAILS

In contrast to all the hardy perennials, woody-stemmed plants, and tough evergreens that abound in spring and early summer, the tender leaves and shoots of bedding plants are the most delicious dish imaginable to slugs and snails.

It's best to have three separate but simple plans in place. The first involves enticing them out of hiding in very early spring by leaving citrus and melon rinds in discrete areas around the garden. They meet for slimy fruit cocktails underneath. Collect them all up and get rid of them as you see fit. This reduces the army immediately.

The second plan is to build a slug-and-snail-free fortress using barriers around any areas where you have seedlings or young plants hardening off before you plant them out. All sorts of materials can be used as barriers, carpets, or mulch between and around plants. The drying dust out of your vacuum cleaner, used coffee grinds, egg shells, copper coins and tape, wool pellets—all are hated by slugs and snails. I'm told silica cat litter will desiccate anything it touches and can be a brilliant barrier, too.

Cold frames must be checked and kept clear of those tiny but utterly destructive little slugs. Use a thick layer of very sharp fine gravel underneath modular trays and among pots and plants. Slugs and snails hate anything that will dry them out or that is uncomfortably sharp, so if you use a thick enough layer or wide enough barrier of these materials and can keep them sheltered (as many are ineffective once wet), then they should work well.

Finally, for individual pots, try adhesive copper tape and Vaseline around the rim. In beds and borders, use beer traps or an organic defence gel that you can squirt quickly in a protective ring around each plant. Refresh after heavy rain.

A quick plea for hedgehogs, toads, frogs, newts, ducks, and other birds. These are all natural predators of slugs and snails, so try to encourage them if you can. Try not to use any traditional types of slug pellets containing chemicals that cast a wide net and harm all sorts of garden wildlife.

APHIDS, ANTS, EARWIGS, SHIELD BUGS, WOODLICE

Your plants may suffer some sort of aphid attack. They could be the sticky black ones (blackfly or black bean aphids), which are often farmed by ants; the pink rosé wine–coloured ones (peach-potato aphids); or the most common of all, greenfly. Whatever their colour, the same simple procedures will do for all: squish, wash, or wipe them off with lukewarm soapy water as soon as you see them. Catch them well before they build up to epidemic levels. Aphids hate water, so washing them off with a hosepipe is good; however, they may just climb back up stems to the growing points, where they are likely to congregate and cause most damage. Organic preventative sprays are the way to go, as these really deter them in the first place. Queen Elizabeth's gardeners use regular strong garlic sprays to keep the aphids

Greenfly can be particularly pesky on the tips of young plants like this fuchsia early in the growing season. Wash them off and encourage ladybirds in your garden, as their larvae are voracious aphid hunters.

off the royal roses in the Buckingham Palace gardens. The garlic smell lingers only a day, but the effect of the spray lasts much much longer. If you're not a garlic fan, you can choose from among the many other commercially available sprays based on natural oils like citrus and neem. I have also used good old-fashioned organic Savona fatty acid soap. It works a treat.

If the aphids are being farmed by ants for their honeydew (the disgusting sticky exudate that oozes from them) and moved from plant to plant, then you will need to deal with the ants, too. Kill them by mixing some boric acid powder (aka borax) with something sweet like molasses or honey, and leave tiny blobs of it along their trails. The ants will happily lap it up themselves as well as feed it to their young; the boric acid builds up in their stomachs and eventually kills them. To most mammals, boric acid powder is about as toxic as table salt, so it's a natural substance that isn't scary to use. What's really great is that anything sweet and sticky laced with it will kill many other nasties—including such pests as earwigs, weevils, shield bugs, and woodlice—that nibble shoot tips, buds, and flowers. So if any of these become a big problem, make a few traps: use a bit of boric acid powder mixed with something sweet, paint the thick sticky paste onto the inside of an empty yoghurt pot or tin can, and then stuff the pot or can with hay, straw, or shredded paper. The pests will hide inside, feed on the deadly treat, and take the bait back to pass to their young. Using this method, I've reduced both earwig and ant populations in my garden to a very low level.

Vine weevil grubs slowly chomp away at your plants, burrowing right into the crown and munching fleshy roots, tubers, and corms during the winter.

VINE WEEVILS

If you don't renew all the compost in your containers, window boxes, and hanging baskets each year, then these evil weevils could become a problem. They will survive mild and wet winters easily in your beds and borders, too. The main problem is the crescent-shaped white grubs, which are about 1 cm (0.5 in.) in length with a brownish head. They writhe around in your compost, eating away at roots, corms, tubers, and the woody crowns of herbaceous plants. I find they can be particularly troublesome on tuberous begonias, dahlias, heucheras, and cyclamen.

You also know you have vine weevils if you spot lots of strange notches in leaves or catch the adults creeping about your garden in the summer: bizarre small beet-lesque things with dull black bulbous bodies. They're often far more active at night, so head out with a torch after dusk and pick them off plants and stomp under-foot quickly. Their bodies are tough, so crunch with conviction.

Turn out pots in late autumn, and sieve compost with a fine riddle to hunt for larvae. As the grubs grow, they get paler and become sort of alien-like with pairs of rudimentary legs held close to their body. If you're a wildlife enthusiast, you can feed them to the birds, hedgehogs, frogs, and toads—or just squish and get rid.

Vine weevils are far more problematic in displays and containers where a range of key perennial plants are left in place from one year to the next. Unfortunately the warm, moist compost in your containers is the perfect sheltered habitat for them.

I often use a biological control which contains tiny nematode worms that will find and kill the grubs in moist soil. It's best applied twice annually to kill successive cycles of the pest, in late spring once conditions are warming up, and again in late summer when things are cooling down slightly. You must keep the containers being treated moist at all times. The optimum temperature is 12–20°C (54–68°F). By doing this routinely every year with your pots and containers, you should avoid any buildup of these common pests.

CATERPILLARS, WHITEFLIES, LEAF MINERS, THRIPS, RED SPIDER MITES

Rolled-up leaves and large irregular holes are a sign that caterpillars might be around. They are often more active at night and hide in the day, so I go hunting with a torch and pick them off in the evening. If you have a serious attack from the more tricky, tiny, hard-to-find ones, then there are sprays and powders containing a bacteria that will kill them. *Bacillus thuringiensis* is a natural bacteria that kills caterpillars, but it does not harm most other beneficial insects, so if your problem is specifically a caterpillar one, Bt is a good option.

Neem oil also controls caterpillars and can help get rid of whiteflies, leaf miners, red spider mites, and thrips, so it's a really useful spray.

In very hot dry spells, red spider mites can become a problem. Check the undersides of leaves, particularly the leaves of climbing plants growing against sunny fences in drying winds. If there are little spider-like webs or tiny orange or red dots visible (the mites), and leaves have a yellow mottling, then it's probably them. In general, insect pests love dry, hot conditions, they hate to be wet. Remove very badly affected leaves and mist over the rest with a dilute organic soap solution.

Leaf miner grubs leave telltale winding tunnels just under the surface of leaves, and whiteflies, which resemble ghostly winged aphids, are found occasionally on the undersides of young leaves and shoots in dry conditions. Thrips are super-tiny insects, much smaller than aphids, and often leap from plants when you brush or disturb them. They are mini-sapsuckers, causing petals and leaves to look splotchy, scarred, mottled, and sometimes almost silvery, as if they have been scratched at.

Pyrethrin is a short-lived contact insecticide made from a formulation of the naturally occurring pesticide pyrethrum. It is a really useful one-off spray, good for killing infestations of thrips, red spider mites, caterpillars, whiteflies, leaf miners, and most other problem insects on many bedding plants. It's toxic to virtually all insects but does biodegrade. It will kill bees and beneficial insects too, so always use it sparingly, just where you need it, as a one-time application, and always on dull overcast days, when bees, butterflies, and other pollinators are far less active.

COMMON FUNGAL DISEASES

In general most fungal diseases—damping off, grey mould, powdery mildew, rust—will strike when conditions get a bit too wet, overwatered, moist, or congested, and there isn't enough drainage, fresh air, and good circulation around seedlings and plants. What's more, if pots, seed trays, tools, and equipment aren't kept clean, fungal spores can spread, and tired old compost can harbor fungal spores, too.

Seedlings and very young plants are at most risk from damping off. This is when stems suddenly wilt, and the plant collapses completely.

Keep the growing environment well ventilated, clean, and fresh. Don't sow seeds too thickly. Use modular plug trays, sow thinly, and space out generously when growing on. Bright and breezy is best. It makes for better plants with fewer problems.

The warm days and cool nights of late summer are ideal for spore growth and dispersal of powdery mildew.

It looks like someone has sprinkled a coat of talcum powder across the foliage. Young leaves can become stunted and distorted. If your plants have dry roots and damp leaves and are planted too thickly—so that you have densely congested plants all fighting for moisture—it can become a big problem. Be generous and water at the base of plants at the soil surface and mulch the soil too, especially in containers. Cut off badly infected lower leaves and have a gentle trim, and increase air circulation around your plants. If you spot powdery mildew early, use a spray or drench. Try mixing comfrey tea or liquid seaweed fertiliser in your watering can and give the foliage a thorough overhead drenching. I also dilute semi-skimmed cow's milk with water (40% milk, 60% water) to make a fine thin milky solution. Spray all over stems and foliage on bright sunny days. Proteins in the milk interact in sunlight to create a brief antifungal effect. Another solution is a flat teaspoon of baking powder in a litre (quart) of water to make a foliar spray. This raises the pH of the environment across leaves and shoots, which stops the growth of the mildew.

VIRUSES

The key to dealing with viruses is to spot them as early as possible, and either don't buy or get rid of infected plants immediately. There are a number of different telltale signs, including strange yellow mottling and streaking on leaves, very distorted and mutated growth, and leaves and stems that look flaccid, as if they are wilting. Viruses can be spread quite quickly by aphids, so if you suspect a sickly struggling plant is virus-ridden, get rid of it and don't add it to the compost heap.

colour planting themes

When you've chosen a specific colour planting theme, you'll find your seasonal displays feel more cohesive and sophisticated and look fresh, coordinated, and well thought through. I really love the challenge that comes with deciding on a clear selection of colours and an overall look or atmosphere. It's fun to explore all the different popular bedding plant groups for the exact hues or shades you want and to choose some brand-new and unusual varieties to enliven and update the mix.

For most of us, the temporary flower-powered displays in our small and eclectic gardening spaces are less regimented affairs than the ones that pop up seasonally in our parks and public places. It's less of a mass bedding out, and much more a case of injecting our borders, containers, window boxes, and hanging baskets with some extra-colourful plants when warm weather arrives or the mood takes us.

I prefer to stick to a colour theme for a whole year, as then a display always looks considered, whatever the season. But even with a continuous colour palette all year long, you can add or take away plants at any time to keep things looking fresh. You can utilise every plant to its fullest and get every last drop of colour from your blooms. Don't feel guilty if you don't have time to grow any plants yourself from scratch. I find I have less and less time for that. This is feel-good, colour-fun gardening; and again, buying plugs and garden-ready plants doesn't have to cost that much more, particularly if you buy only the plants you need and focus on making the most of every plant for as long as possible.

Some plants sold specifically for bedding out are sold in packs of multicoloured varieties; however, displays that are a mixture of every colour imaginable can feel like a mad pick-and-mix that's been thrown together, with each plant in a floral fight with its neighbour. It's a pity. But thankfully, things are changing. Colour-themed packs and single-colour varieties are becoming much more commonplace in our garden centres and nurseries, giving us more opportunity to make clear colour choices ourselves. Bedding themes can be marvellous cocktails of plants, and with just a bit of extra thought about the key ingredients, some tasty drops of texture and creativity, and a bold slosh of pure floral pizzazz, we can shake them into a fabulous and cleverly colour-themed league of their own.

As well as colour, an equally important element in putting together a more modern and updated bedding display is plant variety. By being a bit more free and experimental, and picking from a much wider range of plant material, a more modern look can be created. So stretch your thinking and maybe factor in plants like grasses, sedges, and bulbs, and lush tender exotica or houseplants that will benefit from a summer break outdoors. Strongly scented flowers or aromatic-leaved plants can play a supporting role, giving a display a more distinctive flavour. Colourful varieties of culinary herbs and leafy salad leaves could add extra usefulness, and large brightly veined edible foliage like Swiss chard looks even better than it tastes. The petals of certain flowers (e.g., impatiens, tuberous begonias, fuchsias, nasturtiums, dahlias, pelargoniums, calendulas) are edible in small amounts in salads, so we could also start to view and utilise our traditional bedding blooms in new ways.

It's also time to embrace more popular perennials and shrubs in our bedding out: heucheras, hydrangeas, echinaceas, and lavenders are just a few of an ever-increasing range of popular patio and garden perennials that associate well with more traditional bedding plants. Varying the choices and including just a few unexpected plants adds more dimension and makes the bedding mix more memorably marvellous.

My main focus is always on summer performance, but a colourful spring display is the important opening act. The best colour planting themes kick off with lots and lots of spring bulbs. Plan ahead and plant these in the autumn months, as buying pot-grown bulbs in growth in spring will often cost a lot more and there's a much reduced choice of varieties available. My rule of thumb is to plant a bulb at a depth that's three times its height, and make sure the bulb is the correct way up.

Bulbs and spring biennials go together like tea and toast. Traditional choices for plant partners tend to be things like forget-me-nots, wallflowers, and foxgloves, but there's a much wider range of spring perennials from which to choose. Favourites of mine are hellebores, primulas, violas, and euphorbias. Fresh young spring foliage can be just as colourful as flowers and make a display feel invigorated, too. At the other end of the year, in late autumn and winter, I prefer a more subdued and concentrated approach. I utilise my favourite hardy evergreens (e.g., euonymus and ivies) or ericaceous plants (gaultherias, leucothoes, skimmias) and place generous tightly planted clusters of bright colourful plants (cyclamen, winter pansies, heaths and heathers) amongst them—colourful jewels against emeralds and greens, in containers close to the house.

Whatever type of bedding display you decide on, don't forget to sprinkle a little bit of your own personality on top and be sure to incorporate some of your absolute favourite plants. Stick to your carefully considered colour theme, bring in new plants through the seasons, inject some variety along the way, and you'll keep the bedding party going all year. It's good fun—and with any luck you will avoid a full-on floral hangover and not wind up face down in a carpet bed of begonias.

I hope the flower-powered planting schemes in this chapter will help to inspire and fire your ideas or become colour palettes for you to try out and plant up. Have fun and have courage. Experiment with a wide range of plants and use colour confidently. But most important of all, enjoy rediscovering a fantastically jolly and delightfully uncategorizable selection of plants.

chocolate limes

Many of my favourite colour themes are inspired by sweets, candy bars, and random memories from the 1970s and '80s. Chocolate limes are a hard, lime-flavoured boiled candy with a smooth chocolate centre, and this theme uses the full spectrum of shades and tones associated with chocolate—from plain dark, almost black colours, on to more red-brown, bronze, and cocoa shades, through caramel and coffee tones, to minty and Milkybar white chocolate creams that add gentle lightness. Green and burgundy brown flowers are an unusual twist.

This theme requires a careful balance of blooms and foliage. It could easily become too leafy, and overall a bit too green, so be sure to plant plenty of dark chocolate and creamy white blooms and lots of contrasting and colourful foliage plants. For a contemporary twist, you could tuck in a variety of edible cut-and-come-again salad leaves, or weave in the imposing and dramatic foliage of tender houseplants and exotic tender perennials. The look and feel is fresh and contemporary but calm, so keep this going with smart, simple, and unfussy containers: plain old aged terracotta, deep earthy clay, or perhaps dark metallic bronze. Speckled (not to say macchiato) cappuccino glazes in browns, beige, and creams could work well, too. Both the lime and creamy white blooms will help to lift and brighten up a semi-shaded space, and all the chocolate tones and shades will coordinate well with brick and woodwork. To gently extend the colour palette, add pale lemon or primrose yellow flowers or even a few extra-rich burgundy ones, or bring in more acid green or variegated foliage to turn up the brightness a notch more. Hellebores in all sorts of dark blacks and creamy whites could add extra star-quality plant excitement in spring.

Nicotiana ×*sanderae* 'Cuba Deep Lime'

Nicotiana 'Perfume Lime Green'

Echinacea purpurea 'Green Jewel'

Ipomoea batatas 'Sweet Caroline Sweetheart Lime'

Solenostemon scutellarioides 'Kong Lime Sprite'

Solenostemon 'Gay's Delight'

Calibrachoa 'Superbells Yellow Chiffon'

×*Heucherella* 'Leapfrog'

×*Heucherella* 'Golden Zebra'

Phormium 'Yellow Wave'

Heuchera 'Green Spice'

Hydrangea paniculata 'Little Lime'

dark chocolate, cocoa, caramel

Dianthus 'Chianti'

Cosmos atrosanguineus 'Chocamocha'

Dahlia 'Dalaya Devi'

Dahlia 'Mexican Black'

Dahlia 'Twyning's Chocolate'

Osteospermum 'Serenity Red'

Dahlia 'Karma Choc'

Petunia 'Supertunia Picasso in Burgundy'

Solenostemon scutellarioides 'Fishnet Stockings'

Solenostemon scutellarioides 'Dark Star'

Solenostemon scutellarioides 'Colorblaze Marooned'

Solenostemon scutellarioides 'Saturn'

Pennisetum glaucum 'Purple Majesty'

Hibiscus 'Mahogany Splendor'

Ipomoea batatas 'Sweet Caroline Bronze'

Ipomoea batatas 'Illusion Garnet Lace'

Ajuga reptans 'Braunherz'

Heuchera villosa 'Palace Purple'

Heuchera 'Carnival Coffee Bean'

Begonia 'Gryphon'

creamy & minty white chocolate

Argyranthemum 'Aramis Double Chocolate'

Cleome 'Senorita Blanca Improved'

Dahlia 'Happy Days Cream'

Dahlia 'Classic Swanlake'

Petunia 'Supertunia Latte'

Petunia 'Crazytunia Twilight Lime'

Petunia 'Supertunia White Improved'

Petunia 'Tumbelina Diana'

Calibrachoa 'Cabaret White Improved'

Calibrachoa 'Kabloom White'

Calibrachoa 'Can-can Double White'

Osteospermum 'Voltage White'

Osteospermum '3D Lemon Ice'

Verbena 'Babylon White'

Tagetes erecta 'Vanilla'

Tiarella 'Mystic Mist'

Zantedeschia 'Callafornia Ice Dancer'

Phormium cookianum subsp. *hookeri* 'Cream Delight'

bulbs & early bloomers

Tulipa 'Spring Green'

Tulipa 'White Parrot'

Tulipa 'Green Star'

Fritillaria persica 'Ivory Bells'

Primula 'Francisca'

Primula Gold-laced Group

Primula
Silver-laced Group

Euphorbia ×martini 'Tiny Tim'   *Digitalis* 'Polkadot Petra'

mexicolour

This theme, a riot of flowers that gets louder as it reaches a blooming crescendo through summer and into autumn, celebrates the bold colours and fiestas of a mesmerisingly beautiful country. Passionate, vibrant, expressive. Flowers dominate in salsa reds, tangerine oranges, deep golden yellows, loud exuberant pinks, and flashes of intense blue. Warm bicolour blooms—red and orange, red and yellow, orange and yellow—really shine out. The Aztec-sun-god feel of the bicolours is further glorified by black and acid green foliage. Only richly saturated tones, shades, and hues need apply. Viva Mexicolour!

Some key bicolour blooms are late-summer-flowering daisies, so to avoid a lack of flower power early on, be sure to include plants like alstroemerias, petunias, begonias, calibrachoas, marigolds, bidens, and calendulas in your mix to get the party started. Choose a combination of short bushy plants and mix them in with coleus, ipomoeas, and other trailing types to cascade over container edges. Glossy ceramic pots in plain but deep and intensely coloured glazes—emerald green, aubergine, raspberry, indigo, and aquamarine—will set this bold theme

off well. To add some extra Mexican flavour, you could paint a section of a wall or a corner of a courtyard in a rich bold colour: cerulean blue, crimson, plum purple, or perhaps terracotta or ochre, or accessorize using colourful throws as temporary backdrops to the display. It's mainly a bold fiery mix of reds, oranges, and yellows, but don't forget to inject hot pink and intense blue flowers to mix up the carnival of colours, and definitely add some acid green and black foliage to help melt all those energetic blooms together.

bicolours

Alstroemeria 'Indian Summer'

Alstroemeria 'Mars'

Begonia 'Majestic Sunburst'

Begonia 'Cameleon'

Begonia 'Giant Picotee Sunburst'

Bidens 'Beedance Painted Red'

Bidens 'Campfire Fireburst'

Gaillardia ×grandiflora 'Mesa Bright Bicolor'

Dahlia 'Eye Candy'

Dahlia 'Collarette Dandy'

Dahlia 'Gallery Art Deco'

Dahlia 'Moonfire'

Rudbeckia hirta 'Cappuccino'

Tropaeolum 'Fruit Salad'

Coreopsis grandiflora 'Sunfire'

Coreopsis tinctoria 'Golden Roulette'

Tagetes patula 'Durango Bee'

Tagetes 'Zenith Extra Orange'

Tagetes 'Gem Mixed'

Petunia 'Cascadias Indian Summer'

Zinnia marylandica 'Zahara Sunburst'

Zinnia 'Aztec Sunset'

Helianthus annuus 'Solar Flash'

Helianthus annuus 'Helios Flame'

salsa red

Echinacea 'Sombrero Salsa Red'

Begonia 'Starshine Red'

Salvia greggii 'Radio Red'

Salvia coccinea 'Summer Jewel Red'

Salvia splendens 'Ablazin' Tabasco'   *Zinnia marylandica* 'Zahara Scarlet'

Cuphea 'Vermillionaire'   *Cuphea llavea* 'Totally Tempted'

tangerine orange

Begonia 'Starshine Orange'

Begonia boliviensis 'Santa Cruz Sunset'

Echinacea 'Sombrero Adobe Orange'

Echinacea 'Sombrero Flamenco Orange'

Echinacea 'Double Scoop Orangeberry'

Antirrhinum majus 'Sonnet Orange Scarlet'

Zinnia marylandica 'Zahara Fire'

tangerine orange, CONTINUED

Calibrachoa 'Cruze Persimmon'

Zinnia marylandica 'Zahara Double Fire'

Lantana camara 'Luscious Marmalade'

golden yellow

Zantedeschia 'Callafornia Festival'

Gaillardia ×*grandiflora* 'Mesa Yellow'

Rudbeckia hirta 'Maya'

Bidens 'Pirates Booty'

Bidens ferulifolia 'Goldilocks Rocks'

golden yellow,

Bidens ferulifolia 'Golden Eye'

Lantana camara 'Luscious Bananarama'

Calendula officinalis 'Fiesta Gitana Yellow'

exuberant rich pink

Zinnia marylandica 'Zahara Raspberry'

Zinnia marylandica 'Zahara XL Pink'

Dahlia 'Happy Days Purple'

Calibrachoa 'Cabaret Rose Improved'

Pelargonium 'Horizon Violet'

intense blue

black

Ipomoea batatas 'Sweet Caroline Sweetheart Purple'

Salvia patens 'Patio Deep Blue'

Ajuga reptans 'Black Scallop'

Ajuga reptans 'Mahogany'

acid green

Ipomoea batatas 'Sweet Caroline Light Green'

Solenostemon scutellarioides 'Kong Lime Sprite'

bulbs & early bloomers

Viola 'Cool Wave Red Wing'

Viola ×wittrockiana 'Matrix Rose Blotch'

Primula ×polyantha 'Fire'

Primula sieboldii 'Romance'

Primula 'Fire Dragon'

Primula 'Firecracker'

Tulipa 'Giuseppe Verdi'

Tulipa 'Holland Queen'

Tulipa 'Stresa'

Tulipa 'Caribbean Parrot'

Tulipa clusiana var. *chrysantha* 'Tubergen's Gem'

Primula 'Magic Red'

Tulipa 'Aladdin'

Erysimum cheiri 'Cloth of Gold'

Erysimum 'Precious Bronze'

Primula 'Alaska Strawberry'

Tulipa 'The Cure'

Primula 'Delia Blue Red Eye'

budgies

Budgie blues, fluffy whites, soft greys, canary yellows, parrot greens, black flecks and markings. A "chirpy chirpy cheep cheep" colour theme with a very fresh feathery feel. Needless to say, it brings to mind that park I'd visit with my granddad when I was very little and its aviary full of budgerigars (to give them their full, formal-sounding name) that always stopped me in my tracks. Using the colours of these birds as the inspiration for a flower-powered planting theme feels rather fitting. Granddad would most definitely approve. I've chosen mostly small and dainty-sized blooms and foliage that evoke the colours, textures, and face and feather markings of these cute and curious birds.

Violas are key flowers to nestle into the display in spring; they can make a seasonal return as summer dips into autumn, and perennial violas that flower through the summer could keep their faces fluttering year-round. In summer, Tweetie-Pie-lipped nemesias and feathery-edged bidens migrate to the display and add to the floral throng. Fledgling lobelias dart amongst the bird-like blooms of blue salvias. *Helianthus annuus* 'Teddy Bear' adds a very specific, ruffled breast-feathery feel—lime green and canary yellow is the iconic colour combination of these fanciful Australian birds.

A mix of plain powder-coated containers in the key colours—jet black, ice white, silvery grey, lime green, deep blue, and rich yellow—could really help this scheme to pop. Grey lead or galvanised zinc and steel pots would look stylish, as would contemporary concrete containers in classic clean shapes or simple wooden cubes in soft greys. To help bring the Budgies theme home more clearly, the display could use bird bulb markers and upcycled vintage birdcages and painted birdhouses as fun alternatives to traditional hanging baskets and containers. This theme is all about small, fluttery and frivolous flowers, so "make a little birdhouse in your soul" (as the song goes) and have fun with it.

blue

Salvia patens 'Patio Deep Blue'

Lobelia erinus 'Waterfall Blue'

Salvia farinacea 'Blue Frost'

Lobelia erinus 'Regatta Dark Blue'

Lobelia 'Laguna Sky Blue'

Lobelia 'Laguna Compact Blue With Eye'

Lobelia 'Lucia Dark Blue'

white

Felicia amelloides

Nemesia 'Poetry White'

Nemesia 'Nesia Snow Angel'

Nemesia 'Innocence'

Nemesia 'Sunsatia Coconut'

Diascia barberae 'Juliet White'

Diascia 'Flirtation Glacier White'

Lobelia erinus 'White Lady'

Scaevola aemula 'Whirlwind White Improved'

Bidens 'Pirates Pearl'

Sutera 'Scopia Gulliver White'

Sutera cordata 'Snowtopia'

Sutera 'Snowstorm White'

Plectranthus madagascariensis 'Variegated Mintleaf'

grey

Dichondra argentea 'Silver Falls'

Helichrysum microphyllum 'Silver Mist'

Jacobaea maritima 'Cirrus'

Jacobaea maritima 'Silver Dust'

yellow

Nemesia 'Nesia Sunshine'

Nemesia 'Juicy Fruits Papaya'

Viola ×wittrockiana 'Anytime Sunlight'

Sanvitalia 'Gold Crown'

Osteospermum '3D Yellow'

Bidens ferulifolia 'Golden Glory'

Helianthus annuus 'Teddy Bear'

Gazania 'Sahara'

Calibrachoa 'Can-can Double Light Yellow'

Calibrachoa 'Can-can Double Dark Yellow'

Calibrachoa 'Kabloom Yellow'

Tagetes patula 'Durango Lemon Zest'

Argyranthemum 'Madeira Crested Yellow'

Calendula 'Winter Wonders Golden Glaze'

Petunia 'Fanfare Yellow'

acid green

Solenostemon scutellarioides
'Colorblaze Lime Time'

Nicotiana ×*sanderae* 'Cuba Deep Lime'

Viola 'Green Goddess'

bulbs & early bloomers

Viola 'Sorbet XP Delft'

Viola 'Sorbet XP Coconut Swirl'

Viola 'Cool Wave Frost'

Viola 'Cool Wave Lemon Blueberry'

Viola 'Cool Wave White'

Viola 'Cool Wave Blueberry Swirl'

Narcissus 'Baby Boomer'

Narcissus 'Baby Moon'

Narcissus 'Hawera'

Narcissus 'Jack Snipe'

Narcissus 'Canaliculatus'

Narcissus 'Yellow Cheerfulness'

Tulipa 'Blondine'

Tulipa 'Hamilton'

Tulipa tarda

Viola 'Panola XP Yellow with Blotch'

Viola 'Sorbet XP Primrose Blotch'

Viola ×*wittrockiana* 'Frizzle Sizzle Yellow'

frou frou

Big heavy double-petalled blooms contrast with dainty frou-frou spires and clustered inflorescences. This theme combines delicate, almost antique and vintage colours, with layer upon layer of satin-like and lacy-edged petals. The flowers have a gentle creaminess to them. Peachy pink, apricot, pale rose, and softest new-baby pink, with vanilla, primrose, and ivory white. The leaves and foliage play an important contrasting role, but rather than lots of green, this theme brings in unusual shades and tones of olive, bronze, coffee, caramel, and tea-leaf browns.

It's a frou-frou mix of flouncy begonias, trailing verbenas, and delicate diascias. In borders, snapdragons and other upright plants add height, and foliage ipomoeas and begonias add unusual tones and textures, as do heucheras and heucherellas, with their tiny fluffy towers of fairy flowers. Be sure to plant plenty of foliage in all the aforementioned parchmenty colours—it will really set the flowers off and create contrast. Popular perennial grasses and sedges could add a more modern texture and sophistication.

A soft pastel theme like Frou Frou looks wonderful planted in old tin baths, cooking pots, plain old aged terracotta, and vintage containers—reclaimed chimney pots, milk churns, colanders, a whole range of worn or salvaged containers with a story to tell. Alternatively, use a selection of simple glazed pots in all sorts of rich browns, from walnut, chocolate, and mocha shades to warmer lighter caramel and pecan or the natural grey stoney brown tones. You can brighten the plant mix up by choosing mainly the slightly richer peach and rose pink varieties or totally soften it by leaving those out and using more pale apricot,

peach, soft salmon pink

Verbena 'Peaches 'n' Cream'

Verbena 'Superbena Royale Peachy Keen'

Dahlia 'Dahlightful Georgia Peach'

Heuchera 'Dolce Peach Melba'

Begonia 'Truffle Peach'

Begonia 'Peardrop'

Begonia 'Million Kisses Blissful'

Diascia 'Aurora Apricot'

Diascia 'Little Dazzler'

Osteospermum 'Serenity Peach Magic'

Antirrhinum 'Twinny Bronze Shades'

Calibrachoa 'Superbells Strawberry Punch'

pale pink, rose pink

Verbena 'Aztec Light Pink'

Verbena 'Aztec Pink Magic'

Begonia 'Ikon Bronze'

Diascia barberae 'Juliet Pink With Eye'

Begonia 'Victoria Falls Pink'

Begonia 'Garden Angel Plum'

×*Heucherella* 'Copper Cascade'

apricot, vanilla, primrose, cream, ivory

Begonia 'Truffle Cream'

Begonia 'Buffey'

Begonia 'Illumination Lemon'

Begonia 'Nell Gwynne'

Begonia 'Starshine White'

Begonia 'Supercascade Vanilla Cream'

Begonia 'Kohima'

Begonia 'Illumination Apricot'

bronze, burgundy

Perilla frutescens var. *crispa*

Solenostemon 'Redhead'

brown, olive, caramel

Pelargonium 'Caramel Doubles'

Ipomoea batatas 'Bright Ideas Rusty Red'

Ipomoea batatas 'Illusion Garnet Lace'

Heuchera 'September Morn'

Heuchera 'Caramel'

Heuchera 'Marmalade'

×*Heucherella* 'Sweet Tea'

Solenostemon 'Henna'

bulbs & early bloomers

Tulipa 'Apricot Beauty'

Primula 'Stella Champagne'

Tulipa 'Angélique'

Tulipa 'Pink Diamond'

Erysimum 'Pastel Patchwork'

Erysimum cheiri 'Aurora'

Narcissus 'Exotic Beauty'

seaside chic

Many seaside towns have very colourful and exuberant bedding displays. This theme takes its cue from the more natural colours of the coast—the bright, fresh, and breezy feel of the beach and big summery skies. It's a more streamlined seaside palette, at the blue, indigo, and violet end of the spectrum; however, it still has a sense of fun, so striped blooms echo cheery blue-and-white stripy deck chairs, and frothy white clouds, crashing waves, and the glinting reflections on the sea surface are present in the form of white flowers and silvery foliage. The sea itself is represented by a wide range of blue and mauve blooms: ocean and inky indigo shades, dark dangerous deep-water purples and violets, and pale sun-washed lavenders.

Bring lots of fresh white flowers and silvery leaved plants to this theme to shimmer amongst all the blues, mauves, and purples. To imbue your display with a really clear coastal vibe, use washed gravel, shingle, or crushed cockle shells as a mulch in containers and borders, and maybe dress the set with oversized pieces of driftwood, large pebbles, canvas deck chairs, and a coil of thick chunky rope. You could add favourite outdoor objects you've collected on beach holidays, sailing trips, harbour visits—anything nautical that would give your display your own personal take on a seaside theme.

Decide how "Seaside" or "Chic" you want the display to look. Your choice of containers; which receives heavier emphasis, flowering or foliage plants; the layout and staging—all will tip the balance, one way or the other. To jolly the theme up, choose lots of stripy and heavily veined petunias, dazzling osteospermums, lapping waves of trailing verbenas and lobelias. If you're actually gardening near to the coast, you'll especially appreciate the suggested plants that are slightly more tolerant of blustery salty winds (e.g., ageratums, eryngiums, iberis, nemesias, dianthus, salvias, phlox). I also like to see a pared-down and contemporary take on Seaside Chic, with containers made from recycled sun-bleached wood, slate, or textured concrete—materials that look like they could withstand coastal elements. Add an Adirondack chair or two, and plant up predominantly bold larger planters featuring block plantings of ornamental grasses, scabious, lavenders, and gauras. Same colour theme but a very different atmosphere.

blue

Eryngium planum 'Blue Hobbit'

Agapanthus 'Navy Blue'

Agapanthus 'Peter Pan'

Salvia farinacea 'Victoria Blue'

Salvia 'Mystic Spires Blue'

Penstemon heterophyllus 'Electric Blue'

Lobelia erinus 'Mrs Clibran'

Lobelia erinus 'Hot Water Blue'

Lobelia valida 'Delft Blue'

Lobelia erinus 'Waterfall Blue Ice'

Plumbago auriculata

silver

Convolvulus cneorum

Digitalis purpurea subsp. heywoodii 'Silver Fox'

Petunia 'Easy Wave Silver'

Dichondra argentea 'Silver Falls'

mauve, lavender

Verbena 'Aztec Silver Magic'

Convolvulus sabatius 'Moroccan Beauty'

Scabiosa columbaria 'Blue Note'

Ageratum 'Blue Champion'

Ageratum houstonianum 'Blue Mink'

Buddleja 'Buzz Lavender'

Salvia nemorosa 'Blue Marvel'

Heliotropium arborescens 'Nautilus Lavender'

Verbena 'Endurascape Blue'

Lavandula multifida 'Spanish Eyes'

Verbena 'Blues Sky Blue'

Nemesia fruticans 'Blue Lagoon'

mauve, lavender, CONTINUED

Nemesia 'Poetry Blue'

Petunia 'Surfinia Sky Blue'

Petunia multiflora 'Frenzy Blue Vein'

Petunia 'Fanfare Sky Blue'

Scaevola aemula 'New Wonder'

Scaevola aemula 'Whirlwind Blue'

white

Gaura lindheimeri 'Sparkle White'

Phlox '21st Century White'

Plumbago auriculata 'Escapade White'

Bidens 'Pirates Pearl'

Osteospermum 'Akila White Purple Eye'

Osteospermum 'Serenity White'

Nemesia fruticans 'White Lagoon'

white, CONTINUED

Calibrachoa 'Kabloom White'

Iberis sempervirens 'Whiteout'

Trifolium ochroleucon

lilac, purple, violet

Petunia 'Titan Blue Velvet'

Petunia 'Crazytunia Lucky Lilac'

Lavandula stoechas 'Bandera Purple'

Petunia 'Potunia Purple Halo'

Petunia 'Stars and Stripes Blue'

Osteospermum 'Akila Purple'

Osteospermum 'Akila Lavender Shades'

Verbena 'Bebop Dark Violet'

Lobelia erinus 'Fountain Lilac'

Lobelia erinus 'Regatta Rose'

Dianthus amurensis 'Siberian Blues'

bulbs & early bloomers

Primula 'Alaska Blue Gem'

Primula auricula 'Moonstone'

Primula 'Zebra Blue'

Primula auricula 'Blue Denim'

Viola ×*wittrockiana* 'Matrix Marina'

Muscari armeniacum 'Valerie Finnis'

Muscari 'Mount Hood'

Brunnera macrophylla 'Jack Frost'

Viola 'Sorbet XP Yesterday, Today, and Tomorrow'

Myosotis sylvatica 'Snowsylva'

Anemone blanda 'White Splendour'

Muscari botryoides

Viola 'Panola XP Deep Blue With Blotch'

Viola 'Sorbet XP Denim Jump Up'

black cherry

I'm naturally drawn to dramatically dark and velvety varieties of plants, and I also have a borderline unhealthy love of deep rich pinks, so this colour planting theme is more than a little self-indulgent. It's sort of black-forest-trifle decadent and devilish. I've let loose with hot pinks and delectable berry and wine colours: cherry, cranberry, crimson, raspberry, morello, burgundy, and blackcurrant. Only the tiniest dollop of double whipped cream, rippled with raspberry and crème de cassis, is allowed.

Here's a colourful smorgas-gorge of petunias and pelargoniums, subtly scented nemesias and sweet williams, tantalising trailing verbenas, and of course—and possibly the naughtiest of them all—magenta, plum pink, and damson-coloured dahlias. Make sure you mix the blooms in darker, more intense black, cherry, and burgundy shades and tones with bright raspberry and hot pinks, and don't go too heavy with the black and burgundy bronze foliage. The danger is tipping over the edge from rich and dramatic to dark and depressing. Perhaps

have a few pots of decadently heady cherry-pie-scented heliotropes to really hit home the fragrance dimension, and in any location that is on the slightly shady side, up the ratio of bright hues and rich pinks with sumptuous splashes of bold foliage plants like coleus (e.g., *Solenostemon* 'Chocolate Covered Cherry'). Jet black pots with glossy glazes, and reflective or metallic finishes work well with this theme, as do simple sleek and contemporary containers with dusky dark powdery finishes.

rich hot pink

Verbena 'Aztec Wild Rose'

Verbena 'Aztec Magenta Magic'

Calibrachoa 'Cabaret Rose Improved'

Pelargonium 'Purple Sybil'

Pelargonium 'Bullseye Cherry'

Solenostemon 'Chocolate Covered Cherry'

Solenostemon scutellarioides 'Colorblaze Velveteen'

Solenostemon 'Pink Chaos'

Argyranthemum 'Madeira Crested Hot Pink'

Iresine herbstii 'Brilliantissima'

Angelonia 'Archangel Raspberry'

Antirrhinum majus 'Sonnet Carmine'

rich hot pink, CONTINUED

Phlox '21st Century Pink'

Begonia 'Frivola'

Dahlia 'Happy Single Wink'

deep purple, darkest berry

Petunia 'Good and Plenty Grape Ice'

Alstroemeria 'Inticancha Dark Purple'

Dahlia 'Purpinca'

Petunia 'Pinstripe'

Petunia 'Orchid Picotee Mixed'

Verbena 'Quartz XP Purple Eye'

Verbena 'Aztec Plum Magic'

Verbena 'Quartz XP Burgundy'

Heuchera 'Carnival Rose Granita'

Nemesia 'Pink Lagoon'

Nemesia 'Framboise'

crimson, cranberry

Petunia 'Easy Wave Burgundy Velour'

Petunia ×atkinsiana 'Tidal Wave Red Velour'

Pelargonium 'Supreme Burgundy White'

Salvia 'Love and Wishes'

Dianthus barbatus 'Dash Crimson'

Scabiosa atropurpurea 'Burgundy Beau'

Argyranthemum 'Merlot'

Argyranthemum 'Madeira Crested Merlot'

Nemesia 'Nesia Burgundy'

Solenostemon 'Crimson Velvet'

Heuchera 'Frost'

burgundy, black

Ipomoea batatas 'Bright Ideas Black'

Calibrachoa 'Can-can Black Cherry'

Ocimum basilicum 'Purple Ball'

Heuchera 'Can-can'

bulbs & early bloomers

Tulipa 'Royal Acres'

Tulipa 'Paradise Island'

Tulipa 'Purple Prince'

Tulipa 'Gipsy Love'

Hyacinthus orientalis 'Woodstock' *Tulipa* 'Café Noir'

Tulipa 'Antraciet'

Viola ×*wittrockiana* 'Mystique Black Magic'

Viola 'Magic Plus Rose Blotch'

Viola ×*wittrockiana* 'Matrix Cassis'

strawberries & cream

We Brits have a bit of an obsession with red and white bedding schemes. I admit, I'm not a huge fan. However, I think it's time to tackle it head on and reinvent this peculiar and patriotic colour combo. It's all about exploring the three colours in more depth, as it's clearly going to be a red, white, and green theme when plants are involved. My instinct is to take it well away from war memorials and its "blood and bandages" feel, move on from the St. George's Cross and good old Blighty. My take still has a whiff of patriotism, but in a Wimbledon, Pimms, peppermint tea, and strawberries-and-cream way. It needs a new twist or two. I've injected some edible and some scented leaves, flowers with edible petals, and even the obvious fruits. Deep cherry and rich scarlet red blooms mix with creamy flowers rather than lots of harsh pure whites. I've reduced the ratio of white overall by adding some lime green blooms and leaves and also minty variegated foliage. In case you're tempted, any combinations of wax begonias with sweet alyssum, short stumpy scarlet sage, or white lobelia are well and truly game over.

My tip is to avoid red-orange flowers; stick to rich scarlet and cherry reds. Introducing lots of fresh lime, apple, and light minty greens as well as creamy variegated foliage can be the key to success with this colour theme. Coleus with cherry red, lime, and clotted-cream variegated leaves melt all the colours together, helping to tip the balance and soften this challenging colour combo. Scented-leaved plants, particularly mints like plectranthus, and the petals of edible flowers like fuchsias, dahlias, and pelargoniums add a new dimension that refreshes this colour theme and means it has far more to offer. Verbenas in various strawberry tints and tones can play an important role, filling and spilling from containers and baskets. And why not include some fruiting strawberry plants (*Fragaria*) amongst single and double petunias and creamy white argyranthemums, zinnias, and calibrachoas? Containers in natural stone textures and colours help to soften—and don't detract from—the flowers and foliage.

red

Pelargonium 'Designer Bright Scarlet'

Pelargonium 'Fantasia Dark Red'

Petunia 'Surfinia Red'

Calibrachoa 'Cabaret Scarlet'

Verbena 'Quartz XP Scarlet'

Dahlia 'Dalina Maxi Topia'

Dahlia 'Scarlet Comet'

red & white

Petunia 'Peppy Red'

Petunia 'Designer Red Star'

Petunia 'Stars and Stripes Red'

Verbena 'Quartz XP Red Eye'

Petunia 'Crazytunia Cherry Cheesecake'

Verbena 'Voodoo Star'

Fuchsia 'Sir Matt Busby'

Fuchsia 'Nice 'n' Easy'

red & white, CONTINUED

Gazania
'Daybreak XP Rose Stripe'

Salvia 'Hot Lips'

Dahlia 'Dahlietta Surprise Paula'

creamy white

Argyranthemum 'Madeira White Improved'

Osteospermum 'Akila Daisy White'

Petunia 'Tumbelina Melissa'

Zinnia marylandica 'Zahara XL White'

Verbena 'Lanai White'

Fuchsia 'Trudi Davro'

Hibiscus moscheutos 'Luna White'

Nemesia 'Poetry White'

Nemesia 'Aromatica White'

lime, apple green

Nicotiana 'Lime Green'

Helichrysum petiolare 'Gold'

Salvia officinalis 'Icterina'

Eucomis 'Tugela Jade'

variegated

Pelargonium 'Wilhelm Langguth' *Plectranthus madagascariensis* 'Variegated Mintleaf'

Solenostemon 'Combat'

Solenostemon scutellarioides 'Rose to Lime'

Solenostemon 'Mighty Mosaic'

Solenostemon scutellarioides 'Kong Mosaic'

bulbs & early bloomers

Primula 'Carmine Bicolour'

Tulipa 'Carnaval de Nice'

Tulipa 'Estella Rijnveld'

Narcissus 'Grand Primo'

Tulipa 'Silverstream'

Primula 'Piano White'

Tulipa 'Ivory Floradale'

Tulipa 'Spring Green'

liquorice allsorts

Assorted jet black liquorice sugar candies with yellow, orange, and white fondant coconut and blue and pink sugar-beaded aniseed jellies—I can taste the flavours already. Liquorice Allsorts plays with flowers and foliage in the colours of these iconic British sweets, further evoking the individual candies in the liquorice mixture by means of their look, shape, or texture. The overall feel of this theme brings to mind London in the Swinging Sixties—Carnaby Street, the Beatles, mod fashionistas Twiggy and Mary Quant. There's a looser play with jet black and pure white, mixed with bright blocks of pink, blue, yellow, and orange. Funky, bold, and more than a bit retro. Groovy, baby.

Liquorice-coloured petunias and ipomoeas and coconut white osteospermums, begonias, and trailing verbenas are the backbone flowers of this fun theme. As for the bold candy brights, ageratum and argyranthemum inflorescences fizz with white, blue, and pink beaded-candy blooms, and yellow, orange, and white thunbergias add liquorice black eyes.

To execute Liquorice Allsorts well, you need to carefully stage and style it. Simple but bold containers with plain glossy finishes in jet black and ice white would work well.

A display where each pot features a block planting of just one variety that evokes a particular candy in a liquorice allsorts assortment is a bold take on this theme. Pick only the blackest of black and the purest coconut ice white varieties, and keep the ratio high and in favour of these. Inject the bright candy pinks, blues, yellows, and oranges sparingly and carefully, and maybe toss in some rich brown foliage, too. An experimental and edgy theme for anyone who loves a candy-coloured planting challenge.

black

Petunia 'Black Velvet Improved'

Petunia 'Black Night'

Ipomoea batatas 'Suntory Black Tone'

Ipomoea batatas 'Illusion Midnight Lace'

white

Petunia 'Surfinia White'

Petunia ×atkinsiana 'Tidal Wave Silver'

Thunbergia alata 'Susie White Black Eye'

Osteospermum 'Akila Daisy White'

Osteospermum 'Akila White Purple Eye'

Ageratum 'White Champion'

Begonia 'Nonstop Mocca White'

Impatiens hawkeri 'ColorPower White'

white, CONTINUED

Argyranthemum 'Madeira Double White'

Verbena 'Aztec White'

Sutera 'Snowstorm Giant Snowflake'

pink

Argyranthemum 'Madeira Deep Pink'

Argyranthemum 'Madeira Crested Pink Improved'

Ageratum 'Pink Champion'

Verbena 'Quartz XP Pink'

Begonia 'Rosebud Tutu'

blue

Ageratum 'Blue Champion'

Ageratum houstonianum 'High Tide Blue'

yellow

Thunbergia alata 'Lemon'

Thunbergia alata 'Lemon A-Peel'

Helianthus annuus 'Miss Sunshine'

Helianthus 'Inca Gold'

Gerbera jamesonii 'EZdazy Yellow'

Thunbergia alata 'Orange Beauty'

bulbs & early bloomers

Viola 'Panola Halloween'

Viola ×*wittrockiana* 'Mystique Black Magic'

Myosotis sylvatica 'Snowsylva'

Bellis perennis 'Medicis Rose'

Myosotis sylvatica 'Mon Amie Blue'

Primula 'Danova Sky Blue'

Viola 'Teardrops Orange Blotch'

Viola 'Panola XP Yellow with Blotch'

invincible summer

A marvellous colour theme to deliver a long-lasting and gently smouldering invincible display, full of golden sunset tones and bronze shades that should glow with warmth. Honey, apricot, marmalade, and burnt orange. Ochre, warm sunrise, and barley yellows. Velvety reds, bronze, mahogany, and chestnut brown. Natural stone colours with sandalwood and olive green. Plant the richest orange and yellow varieties you can find for this one. Molten, rusted, and rounded tones and earthy shades rather than pure bright hues. Reds should be fiery or rich, edging towards burgundy. Be generous with the amount of brown, bronze, coffee, and caramel foliage. Invincible Summer will not only burn bright and effortlessly through that season but should melt seamlessly into early autumn as well, when the fiery colours of fallen and falling leaves will only enhance its last hurrah.

Late-summer daisies like sunflowers and rudbeckias dominate the display, strongly stoked by fiery marigolds and phoenix-like alstroemerias. Begonias ignite the floral fire amongst both intense and mellow coleus and glowing osteospermums and calibrachoas. This theme gently builds through the growing season, reaching a healthy and hearty crescendo in late summer. Large warm-coloured clay and terracotta pots look glorious planted up with its colours; they add extra opulence and grandeur to the scheme. Dark chocolatey brown and dull bronze pots would counterbalance the golden yellows. Be sure to keep some horticultural fleece to hand and protect plants from the first light frosts; if you do, the embers of Invincible Summer will pulse well into autumn.

red, burgundy

Rudbeckia hirta 'Cherry Brandy'

Helianthus annuus 'Ms Mars'

Helianthus annuus 'Magic Roundabout'

Canna 'Durban'

Solenostemon 'Trusty Rusty'

Gazania 'Daybreak Red Shades'

Gazania 'Kiss Mahogany'

orange

Gaillardia 'Tangerine Spark'

Calendula 'Winter Wonders Peach Polar'

Tagetes patula 'Durango Bee'

Tagetes 'Konstance'

Begonia 'Glowing Embers'

Begonia 'Illumination Golden Picotee'

Alstroemeria 'Callisto'

Alstroemeria 'Summer Breeze'

Alstroemeria 'Indian Summer'

Bidens 'Campfire Fireburst'

Calibrachoa 'Cruze Yellow Red Eye'

Calibrachoa 'Kabloom Terracotta'

Calibrachoa 'Crave Terracotta'

Nemesia 'Sunsatia Blood Orange'

Gazania 'Giant Bronze Striped'

Tropaeolum majus 'Tom Thumb'

yellow

Alstroemeria aurea

Coreopsis 'Incredible Tall'

Sanvitalia procumbens 'Orange Sprite'

Rudbeckia hirta 'Tiger Eye Gold'

Rudbeckia hirta 'Chim Chiminee'

Rudbeckia hirta 'Irish Eyes'

Rudbeckia hirta 'Prairie Sun'

Rudbeckia hirta 'Toto Lemon'

Rudbeckia hirta 'Toto Rustic'

bronze, brown, caramel

Calendula 'Winter Wonders Banana Blizzard'

Osteospermum 'Sunbrella Orange'

Rudbeckia 'Caramel Mix'

Osteospermum 'Serenity Bronze'

Osteospermum 'Light Bronze'

Helianthus annuus 'Copper Queen'

bronze, brown, caramel, CONTINUED

Helianthus annuus 'Rio Carnival'

Ipomoea batatas 'Sweet Caroline Bronze'

Helianthus annuus 'Solar Flash'

bulbs & early bloomers

Tulipa 'Abu Hassan'

Erysimum 'Apricot Twist'

Tulipa 'Aladdin'

Tulipa 'Daydream'

Primula elatior 'Castillian'

Primula 'Elpiro Yellow'

Narcissus 'Jumblie'

Viola 'Magic Select Golden Yellow'

Erysimum 'Precious Bronze'

wonderful electric

I'm always drawn to and amazed by flowers that emit so much colour, they glow as if they are hooked up to a power supply. This theme brings together electric-bright varieties in a neon summer rave. Acid yellow, tangerine orange, Day-Glo pink, hot red, vivid magenta, and lime green. Have some big polarizing sunglasses at the ready because these blooms radiate and crackle with excess energy. For anyone that craves an effervescent floral colour rush, this tangy theme will deliver and delight, even on the dullest overcast day. It's earthed, it's grounded, but there is no off switch to the flower-power supply.

Bold begonias, both upright and cascading but always hissing with colour, should lead the way, joined by zingy snapdragons and nuclear-bright New Guinea impatiens. Neon echinaceas and sharp citrus marigolds charge the display even more. This theme includes plants that are heat tolerant and enjoy a good sunbathe (e.g., portulacas, zinnias, cupheas, gazanias, gerberas, lantanas, calibrachoas, catharanthus).

Wonderful Electric definitely lends itself to a modern and contemporary setting. These are artificial, otherworldly, extraterrestrially bright blooms. An outdoor balcony, patio, or decked area that is regularly used for entertaining and parties would feed off the intense energy and vibrancy of these blooms. For me, boldly contemporary and geometric planters in jet black and acid green could work really well with this dazzling colour-saturated scheme.

yellow

Begonia 'Majestic Yellow'

Begonia 'Nonstop Yellow'

Begonia 'Supercascade Yellow'

Antirrhinum majus 'Sonnet Yellow'

Portulaca 'Mojave Yellow Improved'

Tagetes patula 'Durango Yellow'

Gerbera 'Hello! Sunshine'

Viola ×wittrockiana 'Anytime Sunlight'

Dahlia 'Knockout'

Dahlia 'Happy Single Party'

Osteospermum 'Voltage Yellow'

Zinnia marylandica 'Zahara Double Yellow'

orange

Begonia 'Buttons Deep Orange'

Begonia 'Majestic Orange'

Begonia 'Illumination Orange'

Begonia 'Nonstop Mocca Orange'

Begonia 'California Sunlight'

Tagetes erecta 'Garland'

Tagetes patula 'Durango Tangerine'

Gazania 'Daybreak Clear Orange'

Gazania 'Giant Deep Orange'

Gerbera 'Volcanoes'

Cosmos sulphureus 'Tango'

Lantana camara 'Luscious Marmalade'

pink

Echinacea 'Double Scoop Orangeberry'

Echinacea 'Double Scoop Cranberry'

Impatiens hawkeri 'ColorPower Pink'

Catharanthus roseus 'Cora Cascade Strawberry'

Begonia 'Fimbriata Pink'

Lantana camara 'Luscious Berry Blend'

red

Eschscholzia californica 'Cherry Swirl'

Begonia 'Majestic Coral'

Cuphea llavea 'Totally Tempted'

magenta

Iresine herbstii 'Red Heart'

Amaranthus tricolor 'Early Splendor'

Antirrhinum 'Candelabra Purple'

Cosmos bipinnatus 'Sonata Carmine'

Portulaca 'Mojave Fuchsia'

Petunia 'Fanfare Royal Purple'

Petunia ×atkinsiana 'Tidal Wave Hot Pink'

Petunia multiflora 'Shock Wave Purple'

Petunia 'Crazytunia Green With Envy'

Petunia 'Surfinia Rich Purple'

Pelargonium 'Fantasia Purple'

Verbena 'Endurascape Hot Pink'

Impatiens 'Divine Violet'

Calibrachoa 'Kabloom Deep Pink'

Cuphea llavea 'Flamenco Cha Cha'

Calibrachoa 'Cabaret Cherry Rose'

Gerbera 'Hello! Magentamen'

lime

Ipomoea batatas 'Sweet Caroline Sweetheart Lime'

Ipomoea batatas
'Illusion Emerald Lace'

Solenostemon 'Wizard Golden'

Solenostemon 'Wizard Pineapple'

bulbs & early bloomers

Tulipa 'West Point'

Primula 'Cupid Lemon'

Narcissus 'Peeping Tom'

Tulipa 'Ballerina'

Tulipa 'Orange Emperor'

Tulipa 'The Cure'

Primula 'Crescendo Bellarosa'

Primula auricula 'Strawberry Fields'

Primula 'Crescendo Bright Red'

royal velvet

This is an opulent colour theme playing with royal reds, velvety violets, deepest purples, black, bronze, rose pewter, and silvery greys. For me, there's definitely a strong regal feel to these particular colours and textures. It's bold, proud, and dramatic, and full of pomp and circumstance. Richly red variegated and almost metallic-looking foliage has an important role to play amongst all the strongly coloured blooms, and it's a theme that can embrace lots of oversized subtropical leaves and unusual exotica.

Fuchsias, petunias, heliotropes, and verbenas lead the procession, punctuated by stately scarlet lobelias. Red and purple trumpet-like nicotianas mingle with ruby red begonias. Deep claret dahlias and blood red variegated coleus provide height and structure. Gunmetal black ipomoeas and pewter-coloured heucheras add extra depth and foliage interest. A careful balance of bright hues and dark shades is the key to this theme; the bright reds will shine out, whereas the darkest purple blooms of heliotropes can totally retreat and get lost, so pair them up with brighter violet blooms and combine with silver and bronze foliage

to reflect light around. Bold new begonia hybrids like 'Whopper Red Bronze Leaf' work well, as the glossy bronze foliage is the perfect foil for the rose red blooms.

In containers, this theme would look wonderful in opulent terracotta and stone-effect Victorian-style urns and pots. Alternatively, for a much more modern look, choose black and charcoal planters of poly-terrazzo, a material that's a combination of polyester resin and small stone particles with a very tactile and interesting finish. To widen this theme out and brighten things up much more, add more scarlet and even deep tangerine orange blooms to the mix.

red

Dahlia 'Bishop of Auckland'

Dahlia 'Scarlet Comet'

Lobelia ×*speciosa* 'Starship Scarlet'

Begonia 'Whopper Red Bronze Leaf'

Begonia 'Majestic Red'

Impatiens 'Big Bounce Red'

160 / COLOUR PLANTING THEMES

Pelargonium 'Bullseye Scarlet'

Verbena 'Endurascape Lava Red'

Canna 'CannaSol Happy Diana'

Phlox '21st Century Crimson'

Solenostemon 'Wizard Velvet Red'

Solenostemon 'Crimson Velvet'

Fuchsia 'Marinka'

violet

Petunia multiflora 'Frenzy Velvet'

Petunia 'Easy Wave Burgundy Velour'

Nicotiana 'Perfume Deep Purple'

Verbena rigida 'Santos Purple'

Verbena 'Endurascape Purple'

Ageratum 'Artist Violet'

Calibrachoa
'Superbells Double Plum'

Strobilanthes dyeriana

Fuchsia 'Voodoo'

Fuchsia 'Giant Voodoo'

Calibrachoa 'Can-can Double Purple'

Dahlia 'Dalina Maxi Castillo'

purple

Osteospermum 'Akila Purple'

Osteospermum 'Serenity Dark Purple'

Osteospermum '3D Purple'

Angelonia 'Archangel Dark Purple'

Petunia 'Tumbelina Belinda'

Calibrachoa 'Cabaret Purple'

Calibrachoa 'Superbells Blackberry Punch'

Nemesia 'Myrtille'

Heliotropium arborescens 'Marino Blue'

Heliotropium 'Dwarf Marine'

Fuchsia 'Purple Rain'

Fuchsia 'Dollar Prinzessin'

Fuchsia 'Blacky'

Viola ×wittrockiana 'Anytime Plum Good'

black, bronze, pewter

Ipomoea batatas 'Sweet Caroline Bewitched'

Ipomoea batatas 'Sweet Caroline Raven'

Ipomoea batatas 'Bright Ideas Black'

Aeonium 'Zwartkop'

Begonia 'Garden Angel Silver'

Heuchera 'Can-can'

Heuchera 'Silver Scrolls'

Heuchera 'Obsidian'

bulbs & early bloomers

Primula 'Stella Regal Red'

Primula 'Belarina Valentine'

Tulipa 'Burgundy'

Primula 'Stella Neon Violet'

Primula 'Stella Pheasant Eye'

Viola 'Magic Plus Red Blotch'

Tulipa 'Black Hero'

appleblossom

This theme plays with the colours seen in an apple orchard in spring, from the sweet blushed pink buds and pale pastel bicolour flowers, pink flushed white, to the unfurling lime and apple green foliage. The combined effect is delicate and fresh, and lots of simple single flowers are used, along with larger, dense inflorescences made up of many tiny blooms, like readymade nosegays. A frothy, gentle, flowery theme, with notes of subtle green and pale pink flourishes, is the result. Think white flowers with pink picotees and subtle green centres and pink flecks and flushes. Lush lime 'Golden Delicious' and rich 'Granny Smith' green foliage should flow throughout.

This theme showcases some unusual new novelty varieties that have combinations of green, white, and pink within the flowers. These green tints, pink flecks and flushes, and ice white eyes or petal tips may not be to everyone's taste, but I'm drawn to their fresh feel, and I'm rather intrigued by them. Some of the plants included in this theme will flourish even if your summers tend to be a little wetter than you'd like, which is often the case in my garden. In particular I find hydrangeas, antirrhinums, fuchsias, phlox, dianthus, lupins, suteras, gauras, euphorbias, erigerons, and nicotianas do well in an appleblossom-inspired scheme in a cool, damp summer.

Like many modern homes, my parents' bungalow has the popular white UPVC doors and window frames. To help soften the bright white, I planted up this theme in rustic whitewashed wooden tubs and pale beige resin and stone-effect pots. All sorts of soft grey, pale sage green, and stone-coloured containers would work well with the Appleblossom theme, as would light-coloured wooden planters and pots.

white

Euphorbia hypericifolia 'Diamond Frost'

Sutera cordata 'Snowtopia'

Gaura lindheimeri 'Sparkle White'

Phlox 'Intensia White Improved'

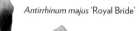
Antirrhinum majus 'Royal Bride'

Nicotiana 'Perfume White'

Pelargonium 'Designer White'

Pelargonium 'Colonel Baden-Powell'

Nemesia 'Vanilla Lady'

Cosmos bipinnatus 'Cupcakes White'

Cosmos 'Sensation White'

Angelonia 'Archangel White'

Begonia boliviensis 'Beauvilia White'

pink & white / bicolour blushes

Lupinus 'Gallery Pink Bicolour'

Lupinus hartwegii 'Avalune Candy Cane'

Nicotiana 'Whisper Mixed'

Nicotiana 'Perfume Mixed'

Verbena 'Endurascape White Blush'

Verbena 'Bebop Pink'

Calibrachoa 'Can-can Appleblossom'

Calibrachoa 'Can-can Double Pink Vein'

Nemesia 'Sweet Lady'

Fuchsia 'Halsall Pearl'

Fuchsia 'Time After Time'

Fuchsia 'Lauren'

Erigeron karvinskianus

Diascia barberae 'Juliet Pink With Eye'

Cleome 'Senorita Mi Amor'

Pelargonium 'Fleur d'Amour'

Pelargonium
'Apple Blossom Rosebud'

Pelargonium 'Little Primular'

Pelargonium 'Palladium Pink'

Pelargonium 'Horizon Appleblossom'

Argyranthemum 'Madeira Pink'

Zantedeschia 'Callafornia Pink Melody'

Gaura lindheimeri 'Whiskers Deep Rose'

Antirrhinum majus 'Lucky Lips'   *Antirrhinum* 'Candelabra White'

Gaura lindheimeri 'Little Janie'

Begonia 'Baby Wing Pink'

Dianthus 'Doris Elite'

Hydrangea paniculata 'Pinky-Winky'   *Hydrangea macrophylla* 'Swinging Sixties'

pink & green / bicolour blushes

Petunia 'Surfinia Green Edge Pink'

Hydrangea macrophylla 'Glam Rock'

Fuchsia 'South Gate'

green

Hydrangea paniculata 'Baby Lace'

Pelargonium 'Lady Plymouth'

Nicotiana 'Lime Green'

bulbs & early bloomers

Narcissus 'Thalia'

Tulipa 'Akela'

Tulipa 'Angélique'

Myosotis sylvatica 'Savoie Rose'

Primula 'Delia Antique Pink'

Primula japonica 'Apple Blossom'

Primula 'Belarina Pink Champagne'

Tulipa 'Green Village'

Tulipa 'Green Wave'

candy floss cancan

Candy Floss Cancan is the Appleblossom theme taken to its frilly and colour-saturated pink extreme. It leaves behind some of the subtle and blushing blooms and instead turns up the pink to full-tilt and massively increases the petal count. This theme revels in pink in all its guises, from sugary sweet candy, cherry, and hot cerise pinks to naughty soft pastel knicker pinks and mauve and magenta pinks, too. It has them all. It's a different, slightly more racy feel, using a far greater range of double, fimbriated, and rosebud flower forms in the mix, with a greater emphasis on blooms rather than foliage. It's dominated by raucous over-sized flouncy begonias, full-underskirt fuchsias, and tumbling ruffled petunias, with a strong backup of peony-flowered dianthus, pouty-lipped antirrhinums, cute calibrachoas, and a full chorus line of candy pink pelargoniums, some with fabulously scented foliage for an extra twist. These plants are shamelessly high-kicking every tint, tone, and shade of pink—here, there, and everywhere—and I can't help but applaud them.

The huge range of pinks in Candy Floss Cancan can be harmonized by adding lots of silver foliage plants; white and silver variegated leaves will work well, too, or, for greater contrast, plants with dark and unusual metallic-effect leaves. You could let all the types of pink fight it out in one big outrageous raspberry-ripple riot, or choose blooms in a specific tone of pink for a more subtle, uniform effect. For a warmer sunset or sunrise feel, use pinks that have yellow, orange, peach, or apricot in their make-up. For a fresher, cooler feel, choose the pinks with a hint of blue or purple, which are verging on lilac, lavender, and mauve. My favourites, perhaps unsurprisingly, are the more shameless cherry, rich raspberry, and hot magenta lipstick pinks. You can lighten the theme by bringing in more pale and pastel pink blooms, or darken by using a majority of deeper intense shades.

Grey, silver, pewter, and charcoal-coloured containers go really well with this or any strong pink theme, so all sorts of materials are worth considering, from shiny or matte galvanised metal to modern fibrecotta, polystone, or concrete-effect finishes and textures.

deep rich pink

Petunia ×atkinsiana 'Tidal Wave Cherry'

Petunia 'Tumbelina Anna'

Zinnia elegans 'Tudor'

Dianthus 'Pink Kisses'

Dianthus 'Cosmic Swirl Pink'

Dianthus 'Scents of Summer Pink Peony'

Diascia 'Aurora Dark Pink'

Fuchsia 'Garden News'

candy pink

Verbena 'Bebop Dark Pink'

Lavatera trimestris 'Twins Hot Pink'

Begonia 'On Top Pink Halo'

Begonia 'Cocoa Enchantment'

Begonia 'Majestic White Pink Picotee'

Begonia 'Nonstop Rose Petticoat'

Begonia 'On Top Pink Blush'

Zinnia elegans 'Art Deco'

Pelargonium 'Fireworks Pink'

Pelargonium 'Sunrise Kristiana'

Pelargonium 'Designer Pink Splash'

Pelargonium 'Fantasia Pink'

Pelargonium 'Pink Sybil'

Fuchsia 'Pink Elephant'

Pelargonium 'Australian Pink Rambler'

Dahlia 'Dalina Maxi Salinas'

mauve pink

Petunia 'Great Marvel Pink'

Petunia 'Surfinia Rose Vein'

Petunia 'Tumbelina Raphaella'

Petunia 'Supertunia Cotton Candy'

Cosmos bipinnatus 'Sonata Pink Blush'

Pelargonium 'Pink Capitatum'

pale pink

Antirrhinum 'Twinny Appleblossom'

Calibrachoa 'Can-can Double Light Pink'

bulbs & early bloomers

Tulipa 'Frances Bremer'

Tulipa 'Fancy Frills'

Tulipa 'Rosy Bouquet'

Primula 'Primlet Pink Shades'

Myosotis sylvatica 'Rosylva'

Tulipa 'Matchpoint'

Tulipa 'Ballade'

Hyacinthus orientalis 'Pink Elephant'

Primula vulgaris 'Dunbeg'

Primula 'Delia Woodland Dell'

sherbet spring into summer

When I moved into my current house, my new front garden had an unusual spring mix of pale yellow daffodils with bright pink and pale apricot tulips, an odd orange pansy, acid yellow and hot pink polyanthus, and some pale mauve aubretias. Clashes of mostly soft pastels with bright zingy hues. I wanted to see if I could make them all work better together. I didn't realise it at first, but these fondant colours were old friends, the pale powdery and bright fizzy colours of the sweet effervescent sherbet I lived for when I was about seven years old. It didn't take me long to settle on enhancing the spring display and extending it all into summer, and a marvellous new colour theme was born. It's mostly a palette of vanilla, primrose, apricot, and peach, with soft mauve, lilac, and pale pinks. The fun is adding moments of bright lemon yellow, intense candy and raspberry pinks, and dashes of zingy tangerine orange. Think sweet soft colours with a few kicks to grab your attention and tingle your taste buds.

I love this soft and fresh colour theme, and I like to tweak the colours and change the emphasis slightly each year. I like the contrast of large double begonia-style blooms and soft downy trailing verbenas with the perky bright "look at me" blooms of marguerites, Swan River daisies, and diascias. If planting in containers, keep to very soft neutral and pale light colours and plain matte finishes. For anyone that loves the sugar rush of spring bulbs (and I really do), you can continue those fresh Easter Bunny pastels, as always, with tulips, daffodils, and violas, and also plan lots of bright floral explosions by planting summer-flowering bulbs like lilies and gladioli in strong sherbety hues and vibrant fruity tones.

vanilla, primrose, pale creamy yellow

Begonia 'Sherbet Bon Bon'

Osteospermum '3D Lemon Ice'

Begonia
'Supercascade Vanilla Cream'

Osteospermum 'Serenity Lemonade'

Calibrachoa 'Can-can Double Lemon'

Cosmos bipinnatus 'Xanthos'

Argyranthemum 'Madeira Primrose'

Argyranthemum frutescens 'Sassy Compact Yellow'

rich yellow

Begonia 'Nonstop Joy Yellow'

Begonia 'Buttons Golden Yellow'

Lantana 'Lucky Pure Gold'

Argyranthemum 'Madeira Crested Yellow'

Begonia 'Buttons Peach'

Begonia 'Starshine Salmon'

Begonia 'Rosanna Champagne'

Lantana camara 'Luscious Pinkberry Blend'

Zinnia elegans 'Zinderella Peach'

Osteospermum 'Serenity Pink Magic'

Gerbera jamesonii 'Cartwheel Strawberry Twist'

rich orange

Gerbera 'Forever Daisies Orange'

Diascia barberae 'Juliet Orange'

pale powdery pink, lilac, mauve

Zinnia elegans 'Zinderella Lilac'

Diascia barberae 'Juliet Light Pink'

Brachyscome 'Surdaisy Strawberry Pink'

Brachyscome 'Surdaisy Royal Blue'

Isotoma 'Avant-garde Pink'

Isotoma axillaris 'Indigo Stars'

rich raspberry, bright pink

Argyranthemum 'Madeira Cherry Red'

Argyranthemum 'Madeira Crested Pink'

Zinnia 'Profusion Double Hot Cherry'

Zinnia elegans 'Cupid'

Begonia 'Rosebud Tutu'

Pelargonium 'Precision Rose Lilac'

Pelargonium 'Fantasia Deep Rose Splash'

Pelargonium 'Fantasia Red Heart'

Dianthus barbatus 'Sweet Pink'

Verbena 'Endurascape Hot Pink'

Diascia 'Little Dreamer'

Diascia 'Aurora Light Pink'

Echinacea purpurea 'Feeling Pink'

bulbs & early bloomers

Tulipa 'Antoinette'

Tulipa 'Honky Tonk'

Narcissus 'Pipit'

Viola 'Cool Wave Lemon Surprise'

Tulipa 'Apricot Beauty'

Tulipa 'Blushing Beauty'

Tulipa 'Ballerina'

Tulipa 'Lilac Crystal'

Tulipa saxatilis 'Lilac Wonder'

Tulipa 'Fancy Frills'

Tulipa 'Sauternes'

Viola 'Sorbet Orchid Rose Beacon'

Tulipa 'Mariette'

bright eyes

For me, this theme has an '80s disco feel to it. I'm blaming early teenage memories and my overactive imagination. It brings poptastic pinks and purples with some dashes of orange, red, and yellow blooms to the fore. These are striking flowers that are just a bit different and ever-so-slightly eccentric. They're nice, they're unusual. Bright bicolours—contrasting light and dark centres, throats, lips, rims, and stripes. They can look like they are wearing a bit too much lipstick and eyeliner; they want to be the centre of attention but bizarrely can feel a little shy at the same time. This theme is fearless, fun, and flirty with a little bit of awkward colourful edginess. It should be highly floriferous with some deliberately colour-clashing floral moments that give the display a fresh youthful energy.

Bright Eyes brings together some of the latest novelty cultivars—wafty cosmos, winking dianthus, bright eager osteospermums, lippy nemesias, and starry calibrachoas and petunias. It would especially suit window boxes, balconies, and patios, where the colours and attention-grabbing blooms can really show off. Mix in solid single-coloured plain blooms in the key colours with no dramatic markings to take the kinetic high spirits down a notch or two and to accentuate the specific bright-eyed novelty flowers and bicolour blooms in the display. Alternatively, up the amount of attention-grabbing varieties, and deliberately pair clashing-coloured cultivars together to intensify the atmosphere. Container-wise, there are lots of options, from contemporary resin containers to inexpensive bright plastic pots or glazed ceramic in pastel candy colours. Whichever you choose, keep to a consistent unfussy theme that's pretty, plain, and simple—the emphasis should be on the plants and eye-catching novelty blooms. In spring, when pink blossoms and yellow bulbs abound, have extra fun with lots of jolly-centred pink, purple, yellow, and orange primulas.

pink

Calibrachoa 'Superbells Cherry Blossom'

Calibrachoa 'Can-can Neon Pink'

Calibrachoa 'Starlight Pink'

Calibrachoa 'Superbells Cherry Star'

Dianthus barbatus 'Sweet Purple White Bicolor'

Dianthus barbatus 'Dash Magician'

Dianthus barbatus 'Festival White Flame'

Phlox 'Intensia Orchid Blast'

Phlox 'Intensia Cabernet'

Phlox drummondii 'Popstars Purple With Eye'

Petunia 'Angel Cake'

Petunia 'Supertunia Pink Star Charm'

Petunia 'Picobella Rose Morn'

Petunia 'Designer Rose Star'

pink, CONTINUED

Petunia 'Peppy Cerise'

Cosmos 'Razzmatazz Pink'

Cosmos bipinnatus 'Sonata Pink Blush'

Torenia 'Catalina Pink'

Verbena 'Pops Dark Pink'

Verbena 'Estrella Voodoo Pink Star'

Verbena 'Quartz XP Carmine Rose'

purple

Osteospermum 'Serenity Dark Purple'

Petunia 'Designer Purple Flash'

Petunia 'Big Deal Pinkadilly Circus'

Verbena 'Bebop Violet'

Calibrachoa 'Starlight Blue'

orange

Calibrachoa 'Can-can Coral Reef'

Calibrachoa 'Superbells Apricot Punch'

red

Calibrachoa 'Starlight Red'

Nemesia 'Sunsatia Cranberry'

yellow

Osteospermum 'Serenity Blue Eyed Beauty'

Bidens 'Spotlight'

Bidens ferulifolia 'Golden Eye'

Torenia 'Catalina Gilded Grape'

bulbs & early bloomers

Tulipa 'Dynasty'

Narcissus 'Jetfire'

Primula 'Stella Pheasant Eye'

Primula 'Bonneli Appleblossom'

Primula 'Husky Strawberry'

Primula 'Magic Strawberry'

Tulipa 'Wirosa'

Primula 'Forza Mixed'

Primula acaulis 'Paradiso Appleblossom'

Primula 'Scentsation Raspberry Ripple'

Primula 'Bonneli Cottage'

a florapedia of marvellous plants

The sheer range of plants that can be utilised in the world of flower-powered seasonal displays is incredible. It's constantly evolving and growing bigger and better, with new series and collections hitting the market every year—wave after wave of amazing novelty bicolours, curious colour blends, and picotee-edged or vibrantly veined, flecked, streaked, and stippled introductions, many with incredible and often variegated foliage effects to go with their flower power. The garden performance and general robustness of the plants is improving, too.

For me the key to it all (besides having fun) is to anchor a display with the best new varieties of classic plants that perform brilliantly when bedded out, such as petunias, pelargoniums, and begonias, but to then mix in all sorts of interesting contemporary and popular perennials, herbs, edibles, and tender exotics, too. With so much choice, the plant possibilities and combinations are endless, and I find it all rather wonderfully addictive.

I've tried to be strict in this book, however, and that's not easy for a total flower and foliage fanatic like me. The plants in my marvellous directory need to be very hard working. They must be able to keep their luscious leaves or vivacious blooms coming all season long. We need easy-to-care-for cultivars in our busy small gardens, sun-baked patios, windy balconies and window boxes, so plant groups or varieties that are beautiful but fussy and a few rather fleeting hardy annuals have had to step aside for more bomb-proof blooms with a lasting presence. Some of my favourite easy-to-grow bulbous

wonders and beautiful biennials that can bloom for weeks are included, but mostly this is a personal selection of my favourite half-hardy and tender plants. Many of them are often perennials, but for the most impressive display they're best grown as annuals and started fresh from seed, cuttings, or plug plants each year. I've also included a few favourite shrubs, herbs, grasses, and popular patio plants and herbaceous border perennials that I'm using in the floral melee more and more, as you saw in the colour planting themes. It's an ever-increasing eclectic pick-and-mix of plants that I fully revel in—and hope you will, too.

In short and in the main, the plants in this florapedia are in-it-for-the-long-haul varieties that have almost super-hero flower and foliage power. With a little dead-heading, watering, and a regular dilute liquid feed, these marvellous plants will keep pumping out colour for months on end.

FINDING YOUR WAY IN A THICKET OF NAMES

The varietal names of the plants used for bedding out and for instant displays may drive you ever so slightly mad. They've certainly taken me to the brink on a few occasions. It's a world of plants and horticulture that plays by its own rules. In terms of correct Latin nomenclature and officially registered cultivar names of popular varieties, it's a real challenge. Quite often, new series and collections of plants are given fun, cleverly descriptive, emotive names, to market them and grab our attention; however, the same plant is sometimes officially registered as something different, or is offered for sale under a range of different names across the globe, meaning the list of synonyms is quite long. In this A-to-Z florapedia and throughout the book, I've tried to give the most useful names, the ones most likely to help you find a specific plant online or at a nursery or garden centre.

Beyond a plant's name, there are certain constant and reliable signs, on plant tags and online, that will clue you in to varieties that are well worth growing. In the United Kingdom, for example, trials are held at the Royal Horticultural Society's flagship gardens at Wisley, in Surrey. Bedding plant industry specialists, nurserymen, and passionate home gardeners come together on plant committees to assess the overall garden performance and horticultural merit of the varieties submitted, and new introductions are often compared with old favourites. If a variety holds the RHS Award of Garden Merit (AGM), you know it really is robust and truly garden worthy. Another phrase to look for? AAS Winner. All-America Selections is an independent, non-profit organisation based in North America that trials new varieties for "significantly improved qualities," such as earliness to bloom, pest and disease tolerance, novel colours and flower forms, length of flowering, and overall garden performance—and then introduces the very best.

Fleuroselect is an international organisation of breeders, growers, and distributors that trials and promotes new ornamental plant varieties. Bedding plants entered by industry members are cultivated on up to twenty trial grounds spread throughout Europe, and aspects of the plants, such as their practical garden use and their flowering quality and exclusivity, are determined. Worthy varieties are deemed either Fleuroselect Novelties or Gold Medal winners, so a variety that has either of these accolades is a surefire bet.

Aeonium

SUCCULENT EVERGREEN PERENNIAL FOR BORDERS / POTS

Aeonium arboreum (tree aeonium) and its cultivars are tender sculptural succulents, and mature plants develop a wonderfully upright and shrubby architectural habit. With their dense rosettes of thick fleshy leaves at the end of mostly bare stems, they make striking and unusual specimen plants or container subjects. They're best grown in a sheltered sunny open position in a display where they can be properly admired and adored. Propagate by softwood cuttings; after taking cuttings in spring or summer let the cut ends dry slightly overnight before pushing into light sandy soil to root. In autumn, bring plants indoors into a bright location. By far my favourites are *A. arboreum* 'Atropurpureum' and the dark bronze-black hybrid 'Zwartkop'.

Agapanthus

RHIZOMATOUS HERBACEOUS PERENNIAL FOR BORDERS / POTS

If you totally adore blue flowers, you have to grow agapanthus. Their rich green strap-shaped leaves and tall upright stems topped by clusters of funnel-shaped flowers are delightful, and the blue varieties are some of the very truest and deepest blue flowers in the plant kingdom. These wonderful and enjoyable plants require very little fuss once established and will often perform and flower even better when slightly restricted to containers. Propagate by division or seed (bottom heat). Feed plants regularly in summer with a dilute high-potassium fertiliser to encourage flowers. Choose from the hardiest hybrids in cold areas. In winter, move pots to a sheltered spot and use a dry mulch of sand or straw.

I love the compact types with slender foliage and sturdy upright flower stems. 'Peter Pan', 'Lilliput', and 'Baby Pete' are excellent dwarf hybrids with light to medium sky blue flowers. For darkest indigo and violet-blue flowers, grow the hybrid 'Navy Blue' or my inky favourite, *Agapanthus inapertus* subsp. *pendulus* 'Graskop'. For dwarf white hybrids, 'Double Diamond' is a gorgeous double, and both 'Snow Pixie' and 'Thumbelina' are cute and dainty, with neat compact habit and pure white single flowers.

Ageratum

HERBACEOUS ANNUAL FOR BORDERS / POTS / WINDOW BOXES

The tiny blue tussocks of *Ageratum houstonianum* (flossflower) remind me of Fuzzy-Felts and traffic roundabouts planted up in red, white, and blue to celebrate the Queen's Silver Jubilee in 1977. I was five and already flower-obsessed. This plant is ripe for reinvention; it's one of the many plants I'm convinced we should all have more fun with. Choose the new violet, mauve-blue, and red-purple varieties; short and dense, they look good in small pots on their own, like little fluffy powder puffs. They also look great planted with totally contrasting blooms in bold bright poptastic colours. Grow from seed (bottom heat). Keep plants moist to keep them flowering. They hate to totally dry out. The white varieties can look a little messy as the blooms start to go over and turn brown.

Ageratum houstonianum 'Blue Mink' is an old favourite and still a good fluffy one to grow. Taller and more vigorous is the selection 'High Tide Blue', with flowers on slightly longer stems. Of the hybrids, 'Blue Champion' is early to flower and stays neat and compact (15–20 cm, 6–8 in.), 'Artist Purple' is an unusual and attractive plum purple, and 'Artist Violet' a slightly paler lilac purple. The new colours are well worth searching out and growing.

Ajuga (bugle)

EVERGREEN HERBACEOUS PERENNIAL FOR BORDERS / POTS / HANGING BASKETS / WINDOW BOXES

Ajuga reptans is a brilliant bomb-proof plant that I grow purely for its foliage. It's a very low-growing, gently spreading, and shiny-leaved plant that couldn't be easier to look after. Several cultivars, with variously coloured leaves, are available. Very much a year-round plant to utilise in all sorts of displays, weaving foliage colour between other plants. Extraordinarily useful. Propagate by division or layering. Grows well in shade, but foliage colours are more pronounced in sun. Keep plants moist. Plants have pleasant blue-mauve flowers, but I feed with a high-nitrogen organic fertiliser and cut them off to encourage more leafy growth.

'Braunherz', 'Mahogany', and 'Atropurpurea' are the bronze chocolate selections you'll see most often, and in good light their dark leaf colour intensifies. 'Black Scallop', the darkest selection I've seen, has wavy leaf edges. *Ajuga reptans* 'Golden Beauty' is unusually variegated in silvery olive green, coffee, and golden buttercream; equally gorgeous is 'Burgundy Glow', with plum, pink, bronze, green, and silver leaf colours.

Alstroemeria (Peruvian lily)

RHIZOMATOUS HERBACEOUS PERENNIAL FOR BORDERS / POTS

I'm growing more and more alstroemerias in large shallow pots in my container displays, and I'm finding it harder and harder to resist them. Such beautiful plants, so easy to grow. I really love the taller types that hold their blooms high and proud on long stems like delicate tropical birds of paradise. Some of the new dwarf cultivars come in the most delicious colour combinations, so I'm increasingly tempted by them, too. The flowers can get a little bit lost amongst the leaves on some of the very shortest alstroemerias, but they do make very smart tidy plants for patio pots. Adorable. Divide in early spring, and allow young plants to establish undisturbed; alternatively, replant the bottom white rhizomatous bit of the stem, as often it too will quickly root and make a new plant. Pull flower stems, as you do for rhubarb, rather than cutting. Overwinter somewhere sheltered with a thick mulch of compost.

'Indian Summer' is a strikingly large and tall hybrid with dark green-bronze foliage and flame orange, red, and yellow flowers. Utterly glorious. 'Etna' (fiery red), 'Tessa' (rich cherry magenta), and 'Pandora' (purple) are just three more wonderful tall garden hybrids that I worship. Inticancha series offers naturally short (to around 30 cm, 12 in.) and compact hybrids with abundant blooms; I love the deep rich 'Inticancha Red', 'Inticancha Navayo' (pink), 'Inticancha Dark Purple', and 'Inticancha Indigo'.

Amaranthus (amaranth)

EVERGREEN HERBACEOUS ANNUAL FOR BORDERS / POTS

Both the leaves and flowers of amaranths are wonderfully exotic. They can make a bold statement in a display, and the multicoloured leaves of many are also edible. My favourites derive from the leafy tender *Amaranthus tricolor*—they are spectacular if given the requisite hot sunny sheltered spot—but there are lots of varieties of other, more robust and hardy species (e.g., *A. paniculatus*, *A. cruentus*, *A. hypochondriacus*). Some also have interesting leaf colours, but they are more often grown for their colourful tall plumes or long dangling millet-like tassels of tiny fluffy flowers produced in late summer. Grow from seed; sow plants in 9 cm (3.5 in.) individual pots and wait until summer is well underway before planting out. The tender *A. tricolor* types hate root disturbance and need constant gentle warmth and bright conditions to do well.

Amaranthus caudatus (love-lies-bleeding), the most well-known species, has the classic long tassel-like flowers in burgundy red with green foliage. This dramatic plant looks incredible grown on its own in pots, so that the decorative tassels cascade and drip over the sides of the container. It's popular in subtropical-themed displays and as a cut flower, too. 'Viridis' is the pale green selection, and there are burgundy leaf forms as well. All are great for cutting.

Amaranthus tricolor 'Early Splendor' and 'Molten Fire' are two hot volcanic red and lipstick pink selections that erupt from dark plum burgundy foliage. Crazy electric colour. Love it. 'Perfecta' and 'Joseph's Coat' have technicolour dreamcoat leaves of red, gold, and green; they are the karma chameleons that Boy George was singing about in the '80s. For a bright lime green selection topped with a lemon yellow feathery breast of leaves, grow 'Aurora'. Finally, 'Illumination', the most colour-crazy selection of the *A. tricolor* lot, is a tequila sunrise cocktail. Fabulous.

If the idea of very thick upright spikes of deep purplish red flowers above green foliage is for you, then grow either *Amaranthus tricolor* 'Tête d'éléphant' or *A. caudatus* 'Fat Spike'. They are ever so slightly slapstick and phallic. For big architectural rusty flower spikes above green foliage, try *A. cruentus* 'Hot Biscuits'. Pure ginger nuts.

Anemone

☀ ☀

RHIZOMATOUS HERBACEOUS PERENNIAL FOR BORDERS / POTS / HANGING BASKETS / WINDOW BOXES

Anemone blanda (winter windflower) is a short gently spreading rhizomatous perennial with feathery lobed leaves and pretty saucers of finely petalled flowers. Plants sold simply as the straight species are often a mix of pretty blue-mauve, white, and pink flowering forms. Utterly adorable. 'White Splendour' is an award-winning pure white selection. 'Radar' has vivid magenta carmine flowers with white centres, and 'Charmer' is a pretty soft pink. Wonderfully dainty yet tough little daisy-like plants that bring delicacy to a spring display.

Equally brilliant but with quite a different feel is *Anemone coronaria*, a taller bolder plant than the more subtle and delicate *A. blanda*. Its selections—larger-flowered, floppy, and usually in strong hues and shades—are also great in spring displays. De Caen Group offers single-flowered selections in bold colours; 'Sylphide' is an amazing magenta, and 'The Governor' is bright red with a white halo around its black eye. Saint Bridgid Group is a fun collection of doubles in a wide range of colours.

Anemones love light but moist humus-rich soils. The twiggy roots of *Anemone blanda* require dry dormancy after spring flowering and should be lightly mulched for protection over winter. Propagate by division in summer.

Angelonia (summer snapdragon)

☀

HERBACEOUS PERENNIAL FOR BORDERS / POTS / WINDOW BOXES

A pretty plant that deserves to be much more widely grown, especially in warmer sunny gardens. Angelonias are adorable; they have short spires of flowers that are reminiscent of foxgloves and snapdragons, and some varieties have the most beautifully spotted throats. They are very useful as dainty plants of medium height for borders and container planting schemes. Grow from seed (bottom heat) or buy plugs or plants and take cuttings from nonflowering shoots. Bring on in a bright place, and plant out only when summer has really warmed up.

I find the cutting-raised types more vigorous and robust. The Archangel series holds well-branched hybrids with a strong habit, big flowers, and glossy green leaves; 'Archangel Raspberry' and 'Archangel Dark Purple' are rich and delicious; 'Archangel White', with its slightly flushed green throat, looks beautifully fresh.

The Angelface series is excellent with some gorgeous bicolours and spotted forms. 'Angelface Wedgewood Blue' is particularly imposing with its spires of tricolour (purple, lilac, and cream) blooms.

Antirrhinum (snapdragon)

HERBACEOUS ANNUAL FOR BORDERS / POTS / HANGING BASKETS / WINDOW BOXES

Snapdragons are among my most favourite cute and quirky plants to bed out. Their slightly bulbous, pouty, lip-like petals in bright two-tone colours are pure floral fun. I love to watch bumblebees clamber in and out of them. The colourful spires of the tall and intermediate types are great dotted through beds, borders, and large containers, adding height; and the more compact, naturally bushy and daintily cascading sorts are great in planting pouches, baskets, and window boxes. There are now wide-open-faced single, semi-, and fully double snap-less snaps; I'm naturally drawn to a frilly funnel, so these have won me over too, as have the comely bicolours. Historically, fungal diseases like mildew and rust have been an issue, but many of the latest varieties are quite resistant to rust and come in the most wonderful range of rainbow hues. Seed can be slow to germinate and a bit tricky and erratic, even with gentle bottom heat. I buy seedlings or plugs to save myself the drama. Nip out growing tips early to encourage basal branching. Deadhead, or they go into floral shut-down. Avoid plants with any signs of rust (small dark orange-brown pustules on the undersides of leaves).

'Lucky Lips' is a pouty red-purple and white bicolour; 'Royal Bride' is a tall, crisp pure white selection with a subtle fragrance. Sonnet, a favourite series of mine, is hard to beat, with its rich range of colours. All are selections of *Antirrhinum majus*.

Candelabra series offers a range of spreading super-short hybrids perfect for baskets and window boxes. Short and frilly-flowered Twinny is an award-winning series of dwarf double F1 hybrids whose flowers last for weeks.

Argyranthemum (marguerite)

EVERGREEN HERBACEOUS PERENNIAL FOR BORDERS / POTS / WINDOW BOXES

I have an innate attraction to all types of daisies, and my love of argyranthemums is fast approaching my unhealthy adoration of dahlias. I love the wafty windy jiggle you get from these pretty blooms on their thin wiry stems. Add to this their perky-poppet flowery faces, deeply divided silvery foliage, and bushy doming habit, and you have a winning combination that leaves me feeling rather giddy. They look gorgeous in containers planted with silver *Artemisia* 'Powis Castle' for an extra helping of leafy shimmer. Propagate from softwood cuttings in spring, from semi-ripe cuttings in summer and autumn. Pinch growing tips to keep compact. Deadhead regularly.

The well-known cultivars of *Argyranthemum frutescens* have glaucous grey-green foliage and for the most part are covered in pure white daisies with yellow centres. I much prefer the more colourful hybrids of the Madeira series, with their deeply divided silvery foliage; 'Madeira Crested Yellow' is a canary Tweetie-Pie anemone form, and 'Madeira Crested Merlot' a deep cherry wine double. Both go on flowering for months. Keep them all well fed and watered. If they dry out, they will stop flowering.

Begonia

SEMI-EVERGREEN PERENNIAL FOR BORDERS / POTS / HANGING BASKETS / WINDOW BOXES

I can't help but champion super-floriferous and ultra-hardworking begonias. I feel they've been dismissed and treated a little unfairly at times, but that's what can happen when you've had too much of a good thing. Cheap, cheerful, tough, and tolerant wax begonias (*Begonia* Semperflorens Cultorum Group) have carpeted beds and borders in our parks and cities for decades. We've slightly done them to death, but in doing so we've forgotten what a fabulously diverse group of plants begonias really are. What's more, some great breeding work has transformed their garden performance in recent years, and as a truly outstanding group of plants for bedding out, many of the new types and varieties deserve to be fully re-embraced. This is a really broad range of extraordinarily floriferous and relatively robust plants that can cope with everything thrown at them, from shade to downpours to drought. I'm particularly impressed by how both the foliage and overall stature have improved in many of the new hybrids. These totally replace the semperflorens for me—they are simply bigger, better plants in every way imaginable. The massive and majestic dinner-plate flowering types are pure showmanship and really good fun to grow, and the nonstop flowering and drought-resistant nature of many of the tuberous and rhizomatous begonias, both upright and trailing, is nothing short of remarkable. The choice of begonias suitable for any situation that requires a cascading or trailing plant is vast, and in terms of flower power they will give absolutely every other plant a run for its money. I may still have to convince a few hardened haters, but some of the new subtly coloured and softly scented varieties should surprise and impress anyone.

Propagate in spring from seed (bottom heat) or basal or stem-tip softwood cuttings; alternatively, take leaf cuttings in summer. Begonias love moderately moist, humus-rich, well-drained soils, but once established, they will often tolerate dry hot spells and downpours. Many perform really well in warm but shady locations where other plants struggle. Keep plants airy and well ventilated to prevent powdery mildew and stem rot. Dry off tuberous and rhizomatous types in autumn, and store at 7–10°C (45–50°F).

Fibrous-rooted begonias. The hybrids of the *Begonia* Semperflorens Cultorum Group have been superseded by bigger, more substantial, upright modern varieties eminently suited for borders and pots. Look for the Whopper series; both the bronze and apple green foliage forms in this chunky, gleaming, glossy-leaved, souped-up new hybrid series are admirable.

The lush and vigorous "dragon wing" varieties grow in a particular direction, as they have an arching leading stem. They work well in containers, hanging baskets, flower towers, and planting pouches but look great in borders, too. Be sure to plant them with the main growing shoot facing outwards towards the edge of the container or the front of the bed.

'Glowing Embers', an award-winning tangerine orange hybrid, has excellent rich dark foliage with Kryptonite green veins. Very versatile and makes an impressive specimen patio plant in a large container.

Tuberous begonias. The over-the-top giant-blooming tuberous types (*Begonia* ×*tuberhybrida*) are huge fun to grow. The bold, blousy, robust hybrids of the Majestic series grow up to 50 cm (20 in.) tall, with blooms around 20 cm (8 in.) across; I particularly love the picotee-edged 'Majestic Sunburst'.

There's an ever-increasing range of excellent pot and patio begonias. Plants in the On Top and Buttons series look stunning on their own in a large container and quickly become substantial. 'On Top Pink Halo' and 'On Top Sunset Shades' are incredibly floriferous, blooming all summer long.

'Peardrop' in sunset orange and 'Buffey' in creamy deep primrose are compact hybrids with a doming habit and large frilly double flowers.

The short floriferous Nonstop double begonias cope well in very dry sunny spells. The darker chocolate-leaved Nonstop Mocca forms, in particular the rich and vibrant scarlet, deep orange, pink, and cherry varieties, are the most striking. But be careful. Planted as a monoculture they can feel uninspired and look slightly plastic and funereal. Instead select a specific variety to use in a colour-themed mixed planting combination. They are transformed into something far more impressive amongst blooms of contrasting shape.

Trailing begonias. A varied group of selections and hybrids (mainly involving *Begonia pendula* and *B. multiflora*) that move into a higher floral gear. They have a trailing or cascading habit and so are tailor-made for big, in-your-face-floriferous hanging baskets. Most benefit from pinching out the main leading stem early on to ensure a fuller habit.

The Supercascade and Illumination series are both prolific. If you want flirty, frou-frou, and over-the-top, these are the ticket. They have both double and semi-double blooms and come in a huge range of both rich and softer creamy colours. The Truffle and Bon Bon series are also fun. Both offer slightly two-tone double and semi-double blooms with larger outer petals and delicate centres of smaller ones.

Semi-trailing begonias. *Begonia boliviensis* and its selections and hybrids are sun-loving and extraordinarily floriferous. They make incredible plants for flower towers, pouches, pockets, baskets, and vertical wall displays. The Beauvilia series in white, pale lemon, and salmon has a compact semi-trailing habit and good deep green foliage to contrast with the gentle colours. Other noteworthy series include Starshine, Santa Cruz, and Million Kisses. Most are naturally branching and flower continually, so are heavy feeders. Give them a balanced nitrogen feed at first, to promote good structure and their exuberant growth, but to support their unparalleled floriferousness, keep the dilute high-potassium liquid feed flowing throughout the summer. These types of begonia will automatically shed old flowers if given a firm but careful shake or a light brushing through.

Foliage begonias. I'm all for exotic and unusual-leaved species and cultivars, including rex begonias, in any bedding situation. 'Gryphon' and 'Pegasus', however, are impressive hybrids specifically aimed at the bedding out market; they have large lobed silver and emerald variegated leaves with burgundy undersides. More hardy foliage begonias are appearing on the market, too. 'Garden Angel Plum' is a metallic, plum pink hybrid with dark black veining and red flowers, and 'Garden Angel Silver' has silvery leaves with green veins and pinky apricot blooms. More are sure to follow. I suspect very wet winter weather could cause them to rot, so I'd still advise protection under glass or a very dry sheltered spot.

Bellis

PERENNIAL FOR BORDERS / POTS / WINDOW BOXES

Retro lawn daisies—it's hard not to have a little fun with that. The comical blooms of these short, easy-to-grow, double daisies look like mini-pompons. I like to tuck the white ones amongst dark-leaved clovers and ajugas in pots. Planted in small but boldly coloured containers, they can have a humourous kitsch feel, whereas scattered widely in a traditional large bed of bulbs with other spring bedding, they have less impact. Grow from seed as a biennial.

The classic Tasso series, in deep red-pinks, pale pinks, and white, is hard to beat. Pomponette is a particularly globular and lollipop-like range of pinks and whites. Both are selections of *Bellis perennis*.

Bidens
(beggarticks / burr marigold)

EVERGREEN ANNUAL OR PERENNIAL FOR BORDERS / POTS /
HANGING BASKETS / WINDOW BOXES

For vigorous trailing daisies that will happily compete with the majority of robust basket blooms, bidens are a brilliant choice. Many are selections of or hybrids involving ferny-leaved *Bidens ferulifolia* or the annual *B. aurea*. They often have fine filigree foliage and sunshine yellow flowers that keep coming all summer long. I rather love them. Meanwhile, others of the hundreds of species have recently been introduced to the breeding pool, so new colours are starting to appear. It's an exciting group of plants to watch, but I must say, it will take a lot to beat the energetic sunny yellow types. Propagate from seed (bottom heat) or stem cuttings. Have protection in place when you plant out, as slugs and snails adore them. Many hybrids are short-lived perennials best grown as annuals.

When choosing a classic yellow variety, think about the growth habit, vigour, and intensity of rich gold or softer citrus lemon you want; the ultra-compact varieties make tighter, more mounding plants for smaller pots and containers. *Bidens* 'Pirates Booty' has fun and feathery semi-double flowers; it is semi-upright, compact, and egg-yolk yellow. *Bidens ferulifolia* 'Golden Glory' is a popular single, with a slightly more relaxed semi-trailing habit; it mixes well with other plants in combinations. *Bidens ferulifolia* 'Goldilocks Rocks' is very vigorous, with feathery foliage and elegant airy stems; looks great in very large loose hanging baskets.

Of the novelty colours I love *Bidens ferulifolia* 'Golden Eye' and the hybrid 'Spotlight'. They have pale creamy primrose flowers with a distinct inner eye of canary yellow. Other exciting hybrids include 'Beedance Painted Red' and 'Campfire Fireburst', with rusty burnt orange and gold petals, 'Pirates Pearl', a charming new creamy white, and 'Cupcake Strawberry', a pink and white stripy bicolour.

Brachyscome (Swan River daisy)

☼

EVERGREEN PERENNIAL FOR POTS / HANGING BASKETS / WINDOW BOXES

These tiny-flowered sweethearts are among the most delicate of all daisies. Annual Swan River daisies (*Brachyscome iberidifolia*) can easily be grown from seed, but the best varieties for trailing, mixing, and mingling in baskets and containers are cultivars of *B. multifida*, a perennial. Delightful plants with feathery foliage. For a fizzy floral brachyscome basket bomb, pick any from the Surdaisy series of hybrids. My favourite is 'Surdaisy Strawberry Pink'—deep green foliage that sets off the rich pink flowers perfectly. Propagate from seed or cuttings. Young plants can quickly become a bit leggy or straggly. Pinch out tips and trim to encourage branching. Plants are perennial but short-lived, so best treated as annuals.

Brunnera

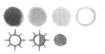

☼ ☼ ●

HERBACEOUS PERENNIAL FOR BORDERS / POTS

Brunnera macrophylla is an extremely pretty and easy spring perennial to grow amongst all sorts of bulbs. Think of it as a perennial forget-me-not, with flowers that are similar to and just as dainty as myosotis but with even more delightful foliage—and it won't seed everywhere. You can enjoy its heart-shaped leaves throughout the summer, too. 'Jack Frost' is the standout selection for me: gorgeous heart-shaped silvery leaves with emerald veins and racemes of tiny pure blue flowers. A marvellous plant. Propagate from basal cuttings. Cut off the previous year's old leaves each spring.

Buddleja *(butterfly bush)*

DECIDUOUS SHRUB FOR BORDERS / POTS

For attracting pollinators to a patio, buddlejas are top of my list. I also enjoy the heady honeyed scent that their large tight cones of tiny blooms emit on warm summer evenings. They are tough, easy summer-flowering shrubs to grow, and the new compact dwarf varieties are great for containers on even the smallest balcony. The Buzz series is very compact and floriferous and comes in a great range of colours. Hard to fault. I particularly love the rich violet, purple, and lavender varieties, as they provide the perfect backdrop for their fabulously fluttering red, brown, rusty orange, and golden butterfly guests. Propagate from semi-hardwood cutings. Once spring is well underway, cut back hard to a tight framework within one or two buds of the older wood. Remove dead, weak, and thin twiggy stems.

Calendula *(pot marigold)*

ANNUAL FOR BORDERS / POTS / WINDOW BOXES

Calendulas are fun and easy, bright and breezy plants to grow from seed, and like many hardy annuals, they perform best when direct sown, as they dislike root disturbance. The showy daisy-like flowerheads are edible and can be used in salads. They will grow well even on light, poor soils. Pinch out to encourage bushy growth. Deadhead regularly to prolong flowering.

Calendula officinalis Fiesta Gitana Group offers short stocky dependable plants in orange and yellow. The tall Princess series, often available as a mix, features fully double, teddy-bear-like selections in yellows and oranges.

New breeding work has resulted in hardy trailing calendulas with masses of small double flowers in a range of colours. One such series is Winter Wonders. I like 'Winter Wonders Banana Blizzard', whose colour falls somewhere delicious between banoffee and creamy coffee. These hybrids can flower for a long time, continuing into the autumn and through winter in sheltered spots. Regular trimming and deadheading keeps them looking good.

Calibrachoa
(million bells / mini petunia)

EVERGREEN PERENNIAL FOR BORDERS / POTS / HANGING
BASKETS / WINDOW BOXES

Calibrachoas are the super-cute smaller-flowered cousin of petunias. They've not been around on the bedding scene that long, but they are quickly becoming hugely popular in warm sunny gardens. These short-lived tender perennials are fantastically floriferous but best grown fresh each year like an annual. Grow from seed or stem-tip cuttings. Grow in bright light, and don't overwater. Ideally use rain water, and let plants dry out just a little between waterings. Grow them in neutral to slightly acidic soil, as they can suffer from chlorosis (yellowing of the leaves) in alkaline soils. Use a dilute tomato or ericaceous liquid feed to keep the blooms coming. I sometimes add just a few drops of the latter to my watering can to keep them happy.

As always, cutting-raised types tend to be more vigorous and robust, and "improved" varieties are worth the search, as they often have better overall plant performance, including more sun-tolerant colours and disease resistance.

The Kabloom series is among the first to be offered as seed; the Cabaret series offers early-to-flower hybrids with a compact habit in a wide range of colours; the Cruze series has slightly larger flowers on compact mounded plants.

The Can-can series is good; 'Can-can Black Cherry' (deep burgundy black), 'Can-can Appleblossom' (lilac pink veins), and 'Can-can Coral Reef' (hot orange centres) are the standouts for me.

Superbells is an exciting and robust series. Plants come in a particularly delicious range of colours, and there're some intriguing novelties, too. 'Superbells Garden Rose' is a spreading type that can be planted as groundcover in beds and borders. There are lots of charming doubles, and they feel slightly more sophisticated and subtle than a double petunia. 'Superbells Double Ruby' is a particularly impressive sultry deep red.

Canna

☼

EVERGREEN PERENNIAL FOR BORDERS / POTS

For height and stature in a border or a real thriller in a container, cannas are an exuberant choice with their exotic-looking foliage and dramatic flowers. They have lush paddle-shaped leaves and by late summer have vivid large-petalled blooms. Those with variegated leaves are deservedly popular, and I think they bring a carnival energy and vibrant Mardi Gras feel to any subtropical display. They adore rich soils and thrive in warm sunny spots. Shelter from winds to keep the leaves from tearing. Propagate by seed or division. Dig up, cut back, dry off, and store rhizomes in a dormant state in a cool but totally frost-free place over winter.

Most cannas are imposing plants, reaching more than 1 metre (3 ft.) in height. 'Durban', 'Phasion', and 'Tropicanna' have incredibly dramatic large bronze-purple leaves with stripes of orange and pink, and deep orange or red flowers follow on to complete the show. 'Tropicanna Black' is a stunning compact red-flowered hybrid with some of the best deep burgundy black foliage I've ever seen. It's a devilishly handsome thing.

Catharanthus
(vinca / Madagascar periwinkle)

☼ ☀

EVERGREEN HERBACEOUS PERENNIAL FOR BORDERS / POTS / HANGING BASKETS / WINDOW BOXES

The glossy apple green leaves and perky bright-eye flowers of *Catharanthus roseus* are the definition of cheery. These are plants that do best in sheltered spots in very warm summers. They love the sun, but as long as they have heat and moisture, they will tolerate some shade and flower their socks off. Grow from seed or cuttings. Plants require consistent warm temperatures to do well. To say they are heat tolerant is an understatement. Keep airy and well ventilated to prevent fungal diseases.

Catharanthus roseus 'Cora Cascade Strawberry' is a spreading, semi-trailing type good for hanging baskets; it's part of the popular Cora series of upright mounding selections that are great for landscape and container use. Valiant is a vigorous new series of compact selections with blooms in pinks and whites.

Cleome *(spider flower)*

HERBACEOUS ANNUAL FOR BORDERS / POTS

The wonderfully eccentric-looking *Cleome hassleriana* is often grown as a lofty annual, perfect for filling gaps towards the back of borders, in subtropical schemes, or for the cut flower patch. The fragrant, almost orchid-like flowers and the five-lobed palmate leaves, spirally arranged along tall spiny stems, make an unusual and striking combination. Spider flowers look great growing among clumps of tall grasses and flamboyantly statuesque dahlias. Shorter interspecific hybrids that are compact, well branched, and thornless have recently been introduced, which has opened up all sorts of exciting new options for using spider flowers in container plantings. Easy to grow from seed (bottom heat), but for the new shorter thorn-free hybrids, look for plugs or plants.

Cleome hassleriana 'Colour Fountain' is a popular seed mix to try if you want a drift of tall and scented (and armed) spidery plants in the full range of colours for a border. The Senorita series offers those shorter thornless compact hybrids that work well as stand-alone container plants; there's 'Senorita Blanca' (in, you guessed it, white), 'Senorita Rosalita', a lilac purple, and 'Senorita Mi Amor', a softer cotton candy pink. The Odyssee series is a bushy and floriferous set of shorter hybrids also well worth looking out for.

Convolvulus (shrubby bindweed)

HERBACEOUS PERENNIAL FOR BORDERS / POTS / HANGING BASKETS / WINDOW BOXES

Two species of perennial convolvulus are really wonderful plants to use in beds and container displays and can be propagated from seed or cuttings (softwood or semi-ripe). *Convolvulus sabatius* (blue rock bindweed) is a subtle trailing plant that cascades over the edge of containers or baskets with clear blue flowers and silvery green foliage. It's divinely delicate and best grown as an annual each year. *Convolvulus sabatius* has both blue- and white-flowered selections; 'Moroccan Beauty' (blue casbah morning glory) is a popular mauve-blue. A more substantial and shrubby plant is *C. cneorum*—mini-gramophone-like white trumpets floating across shimmering silver foliage. Utterly gorgeous. 'White Flash' and 'Snow Angel' are two deservedly popular and floriferous compact selections.

Coreopsis (tickseed / calliopsis)

HERBACEOUS PERENNIAL OR ANNUAL FOR BORDERS / POTS

Both the annual and perennial types of coreopsis make superb plants for displays. The *Coreopsis tinctoria* annual types are very easy to grow from seed and best sown direct in spring. They have really jolly single and semi-double daisy-like blooms with splotches of red and burgundy in their centres. Brilliant plants to sow and carpet warm and sunny drought-prone areas. The looser *C. verticillata* (e.g., 'Moonbeam') and compact *C. grandiflora* perennial types are great for pumping out masses of airy blooms in borders and containers. Propagate in spring: annual types by direct sowing seed, perennial types by basal cuttings and division. Deadhead the grandiflora types thoroughly, as they can begin to look quite tatty and stop flowering if you don't. Plants grow well on slightly poorer soils and will tolerate hot sun and short periods of drought once established.

Coreopsis tinctoria 'Golden Roulette' has unusual half-double bicolour (yellow and brown) flowers. *Coreopsis grandiflora* 'Sunfire' has masses of golden yellow fringed flowers with a mahogany red base to each bloom; 'Presto' is a naturally short stocky golden yellow semi-double selection. And now lots of exciting new colours have arrived courtesy of the verticillata hybrids: 'Mercury Rising', 'Red Satin', and 'Limerock Ruby' are deep rich reds; try 'Garnet', from the Hardy Jewel series, for bright magenta pink.

Cosmos

TUBEROUS HERBACEOUS PERENNIAL OR ANNUAL FOR
BORDERS / POTS

I utterly adore all kinds of cosmos. In mid to late summer their delightful daisy flowers and feathery foliage add a needed boost of colour, texture, and movement to borders and containers. If you get behind with the deadheading, many of the glorious *Cosmos bipinnatus* types really don't seem to care and keep on flowering anyway. The shorter and more compact *C. sulphureus* types (e.g., 'Tango') extend the range into the strong citrus wedge of the colour wheel. The tuberous *C. atrosanguineus* (chocolate cosmos) is rather refined and special; best grown in containers and close to where you can sit in the sun and drink in its delicious fragrance. In spring, grow bipinnatus and sulphureus types from seed, atrosanguineus types from basal cuttings. Slugs and snails love young plants, so do protect them.

Pretty much all selections of *Cosmos bipinnatus* can do no wrong in my eyes; 'Sonata Carmine' is medium in height and a marvellous magenta, and 'Purity' is a impressive, large single white. But there's more. Cupcakes are tall semi-doubles with a unique cupcake-case shape, the outer petals all fused together, and extra little petaloids in the centre. 'Xanthos' is a medium-height early-flowering single in a unique soft primrose yellow. It's a breakthrough in breeding, and I'm sure many more exciting new colours will follow.

Several chocolate cosmos cultivars are now on offer, mostly selected for their increased vigour. These are perennials that can be kept from year to year if overwintered like a dahlia in a cool greenhouse or a sheltered spot that doesn't get hard frost, and all have the luxurious blooms that smell delicately of chocolate. One of the most compact, the dwarf *Cosmos atrosanguineus* 'Chocamocha', requires no staking.

Cuphea

EVERGREEN HERBACEOUS PERENNIAL FOR BORDERS / POTS / HANGING BASKETS / WINDOW BOXES

Cupheas, charming short-lived perennials best grown as annuals, are perfect little shrubby plants for baskets and containers. Many of the most popular are hybrids involving *Cuphea llavea* (bat-faced cuphea) or *C. lanceolata* (catchfly loosestrife). They have unusual flowers with two large ear-like upper petals, which give a mouse-like look to the blooms. These are seriously cute and colourful sun-loving plants that introduce an unexpected flower form to a display. Propagate from seed (bottom heat) or softwood cuttings. Pinch out the tips of young growth to encourage tight well-branched plants. Often a quick shake will deadhead spent flowers.

For a touch of the unusual with a shrubby subtropical glossy feel, grow the curious and perennial *Cuphea ignea* (cigar plant) or 'Vermillionaire', a large, impressive, and floriferous hybrid. *Cuphea llavea* 'Flamenco Cha Cha' (magenta) and 'Flamenco Samba' (red) are large vibrant frilly-petalled selections. *Cuphea llavea* 'Totally Tempted' (cherry scarlet) has a wonderful, more flared flower. Fun Mini-Mouse flowers that keep me amused. I'm more than a little in love with them all.

Dahlia

TUBEROUS HERBACEOUS PERENNIAL FOR BORDERS / POTS /
WINDOW BOXES

Dahlias are tuberous Mexican daisies, and they make perfect plants for border and container displays, flowering for months if fed and deadheaded. Breeding work in recent years has yielded exciting new ranges of more compact dahlias, ones that are floriferous, well branched, and need little to no staking. There is, of course, an enormous range of much bigger, taller dahlia cultivars suitable for large beds and borders, and I admit to a healthy obsession with them—see *The Plant Lovers' Guide to Dahlias* (2014), if you want to dive in. However, for bedding out, I would recommend the compact dark-leaved types above all others and without hesitation. The dark foliage sets off the vibrant colours of the blooms brilliantly. I'm convinced these dahlias are the absolute best to use in container displays, too, where their dark foliage creates an interesting backdrop, against which the whole floral constellation can shine. I can't imagine putting together a flower-powered planting party without them. Propagate from seed or basal softwood cuttings, using bottom heat. Pot on seedlings and cuttings, but pinch out tips and grow on at cooler temperatures with good ventilation; otherwise, plants will become too tall and floppy. Slugs and snails have a taste for the tender young shoots, so put plenty of protection in place. Dry off and store tubers in a cool dark frost-free place.

For the brightest zingy single flowers on dark bronze to jet black foliage, my favourites are the Happy Single, Happy Days, and Mystic series. The Dahlightful collection of singles and semi-doubles are also floriferous and compact. The well-known "Bishop" varieties are a classic set of dark-leaved dahlias perfect for borders and containers, my favourite being 'Bishop of Auckland'. From seed, "Bishop's children" are easy—the resulting plants may lack uniformity but make up for it with a fantastic range of richly coloured blooms and good dark foliage. The Classic series holds taller, elegant peony-flowered dahlias that work really well in beds and containers—flowers with two or three sets of dainty petals and good bronze foliage across the colour range.

'Dalaya Devi' is my current "dahlia du jour." I adore it. A vigorous well-branched ultra-compact hybrid, with emerald green leaves and the deepest chocolate burgundy blooms with dark middles.

The Dalina Maxi series is impressive. Stocky robust dark green plants with large blooms on stout flower stems, and they come in a great range of colours. Look out for them, in particular 'Dalina Maxi Topia' (blood red).

From seed I love to grow 'Collarette Dandy', a mix of shortish bushy golden-nosed clowns in all sorts of fun colour combinations.

For super-small, incredibly bushy dark-leaved plants covered in tiny-tot flowers, search out the Dark Angel series, the members of which are named after Hollywood blockbusters: lovely 'Pretty Woman' is gentle pink and deep magenta; 'Dracula' is a to-die-for deep red.

Dianthus (pink / sweet william)

☀

EVERGREEN HERBACEOUS PERENNIAL FOR BORDERS / POTS / WINDOW BOXES

Traditional scented garden pinks. Sublimely scented, hardy garden pinks are making a comeback. For me, these traditional perennials with tight mounds of silvery grey-blue foliage are truly brilliant plants. Besides being extremely easy to propagate from softwood cuttings taken in summer, they have a good compact habit and such pretty flowers and delicious fragrance that I just want to grow more and more of them. Plants do best on sharply draining sandy and gritty soils enriched with well-rotted manure. A balanced feed in spring will fuel flowering. Deadhead regularly.

A pink without scent is missing its most fabulous fundamental attribute, so visit a specialist grower on a warm sunny day and really get your nose into the plants to choose the most beautifully scented varieties. I have a particular passion for super-zingy, bubblegum, and pale pink hybrids. 'Scents of Summer Pink Peony', 'Sherbet', 'Devon Siskin', and 'Scent First Pink Fizz' are on my ever-increasing list of favourites.

Sweet williams. Of the many types of dianthus good for bedding out, the ones that I enjoy most are sweet williams (*Dianthus barbatus*). Plants have medium green foliage and clusters of fragrant flowers, often with contrasting centres. I love how they can be both a bit retro in a cottage garden way but also bang up-to-date, brought there courtesy of the many new and unusually rich selections (e.g., 'Sooty', 'Green Trick'). Many have great fragrance, too. These short-lived perennials are traditionally and best grown as biennials, but these days I'm buying young garden-ready plants that are just about to flower and planting them immediately, in time to bridge the late spring–early summer gap. Alternatively, grow from seed in late spring. However you come by them, give sweet williams an open airy sunny site.

I particularly like the Dash F1 series of compact, long-lasting, and lightly scented selections. *Dianthus barbatus* 'Dash Crimson' and 'Dash Black Cherry' are dark delicious ruby and deep claret reds, respectively; 'Dash Magician' is also great fun as the flowers turn from white to increasingly darker shades of candy pink as they age. Auricula Eyed Mixed has really big wide-eyed individual flowers that remind me of the traditional sweet williams my Aunty Muriel loved to grow.

Diascia (twinspur)

SEMI-EVERGREEN HERBACEOUS PERENNIAL FOR BORDERS /
POTS / HANGING BASKETS / WINDOW BOXES

Diascia is a genus of around seventy species from South Africa. The common name of these dainty plants is twinspur, a reference to the two adorable little horns at the back of each flower. The blooms are delicately arranged along little racemes and spires. To simplify what is a complex range of species and cultivars into two general looks: there are stocky, rigid, erect-flowering types that make great plants for borders and large containers, and slightly looser, mounding, and gently trailing types that are brilliant for containers, baskets, and window boxes. All are utterly charming. Grow from seed or softwood cuttings. Plants can get straggly and benefit from a short sharp haircut to keep them in shape after each flush of flower.

Flirtation is a very floriferous collection of compact and early-to-flower hybrids with large flowers. The hybrids of the Aurora series are smart, upright, heat-tolerant, and likewise totally floriferous; sometimes marketed as "Towers of Flowers," plants have masses of sturdy triangular flower spikes up to around 30 cm (12 in.) tall. The Little series offers frothy, mounding, sterile hybrids that flower for an incredibly long time; perfect for baskets and window boxes. The Juliet range, selections of *Diascia barberae*, offers slightly bigger flowers, and some have a darker throat, giving each bloom a delightful eye; great for baskets and planting pouches.

Dichondra (ponysfoot)

SEMI-EVERGREEN HERBACEOUS PERENNIAL FOR BORDERS /
POTS / HANGING BASKETS / WINDOW BOXES

Dichondra argentea 'Silver Falls' is my favourite silver-leaved plant to cascade over the edge of containers and hang elegantly from baskets. It works beautifully well in window boxes or planting pouches. Recently I've also started to use *D. sericea* 'Emerald Falls', which is a lush apple green. Few delicate trailing foliage plants are quite as good as these two. Plants are perennial but best refreshed each year. Propagate by seed or layering, although the latter can be tricky. Securely pin down stems either side of a leaf node to the soil surface, and keep gently moist. Stems should root in about six weeks and can then be cut from the mother plant. Be careful not to overwater at first.

Digitalis (foxglove)

SEMI-EVERGREEN HERBACEOUS PERENNIAL OR BIENNIAL
FOR BORDERS / POTS

Foxgloves are either biennials or short-lived perennials, with rosettes of soft, hairy leaves and wonderfully tall, one-sided spires of pendant, tubular, pixie-hat flowers. Some have beautiful dotty throat markings that act as nectar guides for the bees, which seem to be enraptured by them. They are marvellous plants, and once you start growing them you'll probably never stop. The popular hardy biennials derived from *Digitalis purpurea* are some of the best plants to bridge the slight floral gap that can occur between the end of spring and the beginning of summer. Recent breeding work between *D. purpurea* and the more tender, short-lived perennial *D. canariensis* has yielded all sorts of exciting new hybrids. Grow from seed. Purpurea types love humus-rich soil in partial shade, ideally, but they will grow pretty much anywhere. Some plants can produce thousands of seeds, so deadhead after flowering unless you want plants to seed themselves everywhere, or choose some of the modern sterile hybrids.

I love the taller full-height foxgloves best of all. *Digitalis purpurea* 'Sutton's Apricot' is a favourite. Gorgeous gentle peachy pink flowers on tall stems. Glittering Prizes Group, another purpurea selection, is a fun blotch-tastic vintage mix if you want big individual dotty blooms and plants with a chocolate-box cottage feel; their loaded heavy spires will need supporting, however.

Polkadot foxgloves are exciting new sterile hybrids that can be raised from seed. Their tightly packed spires of flowers come in the most sumptuous colours with brilliant blotching, and they bloom over a very long period. They're fast becoming my favourites.

Digitalis purpurea subsp. *heywoodii* 'Silver Fox' and other silver-leaved varieties could be a new craze; their white flowers are fabulous.

Echinacea (coneflower)

HERBACEOUS PERENNIAL FOR BORDERS / POTS

I see echinaceas as perfect medium-height herbaceous perennials to incorporate into all sorts of displays, and the colourful and showy hybrids are currently the height of fashion. I can't get enough of the zingy prickly cones and thin ribbon-like petals of the singles or the feathery powder-puffy doubles in late summer. They're becoming addictive. Propagate by division, seed, or basal cuttings. Keep plants on the dry side over the winter months, as they can suffer from root and crown rot in prolonged cold wet weather.

Among the singles, I love the shorter large-flowered *Echinacea purpurea* 'Green Jewel' and the Sombrero series of zingy hybrids, which are well branched, compact, and great for containers, as they're not too tall. 'Sombrero Salsa Red' is a glorious saucy tangy tomato, but the oranges ('Sombrero Adobe Orange', 'Sombrero Flamenco Orange') are great, too. I just love them all.

The doubles are a different thing altogether. No clean central prickly boss in these coneflowers—instead, a sort of puffed-up mound of petals like a brooding bird's fluffy breast of feathers. The Double Scoop series is an intensely colourful range of feathery-petalled hybrids; rich 'Double Scoop Cranberry' and tangerine-pink 'Double Scoop Orangeberry' are standouts.

Erigeron
(*Mexican fleabane / Spanish daisy*)

HERBACEOUS PERENNIAL FOR BORDERS / POTS / HANGING
BASKETS / WINDOW BOXES

Erigeron karvinskianus is an adorable easy-to-grow daisy. Its sprawling growth habit makes it perfect for lots of situations—one is the thinnest soil imaginable, around the edge of my friend Laura's log cabin, where it grows in a frothy haze. It can self-seed, colonising slopes, crevices, walls, and paving, and spills and fills in beautifully around larger plants in containers. Masses of small white daisies turn pink as they mature. Simply gorgeous. 'Stallone', 'Kew Profusion', 'Spindrift', and 'Sea of Blossom' are the selections most often seen. All incredibly similar floriferous plants. However, the vigorous and robust straight species is hard to beat. Grow from seed. Can become slightly invasive in warm gardens.

Eryngium (*sea holly*)

HERBACEOUS PERENNIAL FOR BORDERS / POTS

Eryngiums with their steely blue thistle-like flowers and rigid stems add instant interest and architecture to a display and keep on giving as they die and turn silvery brown. These deservedly popular perennials look wonderful with grasses, rushes, and sedges but can also be paired with all sorts of plants that enjoy a warm, sunny, and sharply draining situation. Propagate by division, root cuttings, or seed. Plants love gritty, sandy but fertile sites. In very wet winters they can struggle and rot, so a dry, sheltered place is best—and give them a dry mulch of gravel.

'Blue Hobbit', a naturally short and compact blue form of *Eryngium planum*, is great for containers. Silvery blue stems and flowers that turn from green to steely metallic blue. *Eryngium leavenworthii* can be grown from seed and will flower in its first year. *Eryngium alpinum* 'Blue Lace' has possibly the most lace-like violet-blue flowerheads of all.

Erysimum (wallflower)

EVERGREEN HERBACEOUS PERENNIAL FOR BORDERS / POTS

An explosion of breeding work has resulted in some fantastic repeat-flowering erysimums in gorgeous colour combinations; these new hybrids, often referred to as patio wallflowers, are brilliant plants that seem to keep on flowering almost all year round, and some have good scent. However, traditional wallflowers (*Erysimum cheiri* and its forms), which are often grown as biennials, have also improved and overall can be slightly more substantial plants. What's more, they emit one of the most wonderfully powerful fragrances in my spring garden, so I must have some of both types. Most erysimums are short-lived perennials, even though they're often grown as biennials. It's the tradition to buy inexpensive plants in bundles in autumn to plant amongst bulbs, enjoy the show in spring, and then discard. This helps prevent buildup of the soil pathogen that causes clubroot, a disease to which wallflowers are rather susceptible. As plants, they all tend to get a bit lanky, loose, and scruffy after their first year, so it's good to trim to lowest shoots after flowering and to totally refresh stands by regularly repropagating. Propagate from short, nonflowering, semi-ripe cuttings taken in spring or summer.

Traditional wallflowers are easy to raise from seed, and as plants they are inexpensive to buy from farmers' markets and nurseries in the autumn months. There are vigorous and sterile F1 hybrids as well as colourful open-pollinated mixtures that are less uniform but often slightly cheaper. My favourites are the very dark rich varieties like *Erysimum cheiri* 'Vulcan', a devilishly dark purple crimson.

Among the patio wallflowers is 'Apricot Twist', a slightly shorter compact hybrid whose fragrant flowers emerge from dark purplish buds and then turn from golden satsuma to bronzy burnt orange. 'Precious Bronze' has burgundy buds that open to a deep golden yellow, and 'Pastel Patchwork' has fruit salad flowers that turn from pale pineapple to peachy pink. Delicious.

Eschscholzia (*California poppy*)

HERBACEOUS ANNUAL FOR BORDERS / POTS

Eschscholzia californica and its selections are vibrant, easy-to-grow annual poppies, and if you have a bare patch of soil in good sun, these are a great bet. The finely filigree grey-blue foliage is deeply cut, and the papery flowers shimmer and shine above it. California poppies often grow best in very light, free-draining soils. Young plants quickly develop a fleshy taproot and soft floppy stems, so it's best to direct sow seed in autumn or spring where you want them to bloom. The seedpods are attractive and the same colour as the foliage, but plants will keep flowering longer if you deadhead.

The classic pure tangerine dream of the species is unbeatable; however, it is well worth exploring the other colours. The white selections (e.g., 'Alba' and the more icy 'Ivory Castle') are gorgeous, and the blooms of the pink varieties especially work really well with the glaucous foliage. *Eschscholzia californica* 'Cherry Swirl' has frilly semi- to fully double flowers in rich cherry red with golden centres.

Eucomis (*pineapple lily*)

PERENNIAL BULB FOR BORDERS / POTS

Eucomis are South African summer-flowering bulbs that can really add an enlivening dash of the unusual and unexpected to a display in late summer. They have basal rosettes of leaves with stocky stems covered in starry flowers and a strange tuft of leafy bracts at the top. Bizarre and beautiful, eccentric and exotic, but these pineapple-like plants are more robust than they appear and great fun to grow. Plant bulbs deeply with a handful of grit underneath for extra drainage. Protect leaves from slugs as they emerge in late spring. Don't deadhead: they look almost as amazing in seed as they do in flower and will provide interest well into autumn. Remove top growth when it turns yellow and mushy. Mulch generously, or put plants in a dry sheltered spot.

Eucomis bicolor is the classic species with pale ivory green flowers, each finely edged in plum purple as if individually painted. *Eucomis comosa* 'Sparkling Burgundy' has stunning dark cherry burgundy flowers and foliage, the latter eventually turning olive brown. 'Tugela Jade' is a creamy lime green hybrid I fell deeply in love with at the Kirstenbosch National Botanical Garden in Cape Town. Magnificently marvellous.

Euphorbia (spurge)

●●●●●●
☼ ☼

HERBACEOUS PERENNIAL FOR BORDERS / POTS

Wonderfully varied and versatile groups of plants like euphorbias are now playing an important part in bedding out and container displays. Many are widely available as small young plants, and of these it's often the shorter compact selections and hybrids of *Euphorbia* ×*martini*, *E. amygdaloides*, *E. cyparissias*, and *E. epithymoides* that are the most useful. The grey-blue, almost succulent-leaved types like full sun and well-drained spots. Lush green-leaved types will cope in semi-shade; most are forms of *E. amygdaloides* and *E.* ×*martini*. All euphorbias are sappy. Wear gloves when handling, as the milky latex the plants exude can irritate skin. Dip the cut ends of cuttings in ground charcoal; this helps to seal and stop loss of moisture. Propagate by seed or division in early spring, basal cuttings in early summer.

Euphorbia amygdaloides 'Purpurea' is widely available and reliable, with gorgeous dark foliage, beetroot stems, and acid green bracts.

Euphorbia ×*martini* 'Tiny Tim' is a small tight compact hybrid with fresh green foliage that is blushed burgundy on the undersides and stems.

Euphorbia epithymoides cultivars are early to flower and will stay short and compact. 'Bonfire' is a brilliant selection: sulphur yellow bracts above foliage that turns from green to plum burgundy in the summer and then burns up into bright red in autumn.

Euphorbia cyparissias 'Fens Ruby' supplies a glaucous blue-green and acid green combination that you can only really get from euphorbias—and this one has ruby red tips. It can spread everywhere, so grow in a container ideally.

Euphorbia rigida is a spreading evergreen grey-blue perennial with fleshy stegosaurus-like spirally arranged leaves; it loves sharply draining soils and full sun.

The more tender *Euphorbia hypericifolia* has recently provided lots of frothy white delicate-flowered cultivars that are extremely popular in container displays, and rightly so. Grown as tender perennials, they flower relentlessly through spring and summer and into autumn, and once established can withstand heat and drought and will even tolerate slightly salty seaside conditions. 'Diamond Frost' is a medium-sized selection, an airy cloud of white flowers.

Felicia
(blue marguerite / kingfisher daisy)

⬤ ◯
☀

EVERGREEN HERBACEOUS PERENNIAL FOR BORDERS / POTS /
HANGING BASKETS / WINDOW BOXES

Felicia amelloides is a sky blue South African daisy that effortlessly combines "pretty" with "robust." Flowers have fine blue-mauve petals and bright yellow button centres, and the foliage is small and slightly leathery. This tough little plant will cope well in very hot sunny locations once established. My favourite variety, 'Santa Anita', has larger flowers and glossy green leaves. 'Santa Anita Variegated' has creamy white variegation. There are white-flowering forms, but for me the joy of this wonderful daisy is its sky blue petals. A perennial, but best grown as a half-hardy annual. Overwinter plants under glass and water sparingly; propagate by taking stem-tip softwood cuttings in spring and summer.

Fritillaria (fritillary)

◖ ◐ ◯ ▥ ⬤ ⬤ ◯ ◯
☀ ☼

PERENNIAL BULB FOR BORDERS / POTS /
WINDOW BOXES

Fritillaries are bulbous plants closely related to lilies; they have graceful nodding, bell-shaped flowers and come in some unusual burgundy and cream colours. They can be a really interesting and unusual addition to a spring display. Relatively few of the well over a hundred species are very widely available and vigorous enough for bedding displays. But even among that select group, I do have my favourites, from the popular purple and white *Fritillaria meleagris* (snake's head fritillary) to more tall and substantial types like *F. raddeana*, which has gorgeous pale lime yellow flowers similar to the more commonly grown *F. imperialis* (crown imperial). My absolute favourite, *F. persica* (Persian lily), likes a warm summer baking and very sharp drainage, ideally; 'Ivory Bells' is an incredibly showy selection with a mass of pendant bell-shaped soft greenish ivory flowers on stocky stalks above wavy, glaucous green foliage. Plant bulbs on their side on a handful of grit to ensure good drainage around the bulb. Propagate from offsets or seed.

Fuchsia

PERENNIAL SHRUB FOR BORDERS / POTS /
HANGING BASKETS / WINDOW BOXES

After just two summer seasons of rediscovering one of my granddad's favourite plants, and growing a range of different varieties, I'm a totally born-again and positively evangelical fuchsia lover. These plants have blown me away in terms of their sheer floriferousness, and I've rathered enjoyed deadheading them every few days. It's important to commit to this if you do grow them, as they will perform so much better and flower continuously rather than in flushes and lulls.

The majority of cultivated types have the classic hanging bell-shaped flowers with four swept-back petals at the top, and below a group of petals forming a bell. For me, it's hard to beat that classic single flower form, with its very long elegant stigma and stamens. However, there are some pretty incredible double forms; some are extraordinarily big, with a full underskirt of swirly petals that are super-crazy frou-frou. A contender for the title of the campiest thing ever seen hanging from a branch, these giant blooms are plus-size with attitude—both awe-inspiringly beautiful and hilarious at the same time.

Quite different from these are the cluster-flowered types derived from *Fuchsia triphylla*. These are slightly more elegant and exotic-looking plants, a few steps away from the better-known floral campery. These elegant fuchsias have flowers that resemble long thin tubes with short stiffly held sepals at the end. They often have slightly darker coloured foliage, which sets off the flowers perfectly. They can take a hot position in full sun in summer but are very frost tender so require protection during winter in a light gently heated place. Unlike the other types, stems can all be cut back hard in late autumn to about 10 cm (4 in.).

Oddly enough for bedding plants, fuchsias look their very best viewed from below. The more lax trailing types, with very large trusses of flowers, come into their own in elevated or hanging situations, where you can really look up or across and appreciate the blooms; and even the more-upright plants can feel a little lost planted in the ground. It's traditional, therefore, to grow standard fuchsias—that is, plants where the main stem has been trained and side shoots pinched out until the specimen reaches the desired height. Sort of lollipop fuchsia trees. These can look rather wonderful in more formal gardens that have good ever-present evergreen structure and a strong symmetrical layout.

Traditionally many bedding type fuchsias were tender varieties that were killed by frosts; however, there's no reason why any one of them, from the hardy types to the tender, can't be used in displays. I always choose for colour first but try to include a few of the hardier types, as I have limited overwintering space under glass. As with any plant group, hardiness is very much a sliding scale and can be different from one garden to the next. I view any plants that make it through the winter as a bonus. Propagate from cuttings (softwood or semi-ripe). If you want to grow a standard fuchsia, buy plugs or plants that are unpinched. Plants hate to completely dry out. Keep well watered and feed with a dilute liquid high-potassium feed through the summer. Deadhead regularly!

Well over a hundred varieties currently hold an RHS Award of Garden Merit, but there are hundreds upon hundreds of amazing cultivars and species. Again, for me—first, foremost, and always—it's all about colour. Fuchsia blooms are often bicolours, and the colours of the upper tube and sepals and lower corolla of petals all need to coordinate in a display, so combine carefully. I love the deep and rich bicolours best—deep purples and violets with rich reds and magentas being classic combinations I'm very keen on indeed. I also love fuchsias for their amazing range of pinks, from darker shades through bubblegum and candy floss pinks to soft pastel blushes and very palest appleblossom to almost pure white; I totally adore the midrange lipstick pink fuchsias, but must admit I find the tinned-red-salmon or lilac mauve varieties harder to love.

Secondly it's about habit and hardiness. The hardy, shrubby and upright bushy types look good in borders and containers, where they'll add volume, structure, and height, and they work well on patios as perfect potted floriferous wonders. Those with lax trailing and semi-trailing growth and the ones with more sturdy arching stems are wonderful for big baskets, planting pouches, and tall containers—anywhere high up where the plants can literally let it all hang out and you can really see those amazing blooms. The more fuchsias I grow, the more I realise I'm about to turn into a bit of a fuchsia fiend. Such floriferous and enjoyable plants to grow. I'm already slightly obsessed.

Hardy fuchsias. Hardy types will often grow most vigorously planted in the ground. If they are grown in pots, some may need a more sheltered site to overwinter successfully. Always leave the whole dead woody structure on the plant throughout the winter, and in late spring, once the last frosts have passed, cut back to just above the strongest lowest buds, leaving a short open framework for regrowth. 'Garden News'—with frosty pink top sepals and a deep double cherry magenta bell underneath—is a sugary pink favourite. Another hardy favourite is 'Dollar Prinzessin', a classic rich red and deep purple AGM.

Upright/bush fuchsias. These will need frost protection during the winter months, ideally in a cool but frost-free greenhouse. They are an excellent versatile choice for summer displays. For pretty poppet single flowers, grow 'Halsall Pearl'; it's a very pale blush pink, with a distinct hint of green on the buds and tips of the top petals. 'Purple Rain' is a good single with corollas that open very dark purple, maturing to deep red. There are some stunning doubles and semi-doubles too, such as 'Blacky', with cherry pink sepals and plum purple under-petals.

Trailing/basket fuchsias. These often have a lax growth habit or long, strongly arching growth, so are perfect for hanging baskets, or for cascading over the sides of tall pots. Pinching out shoot tips early on will help develop a well-branched plant. They require protection from frost during the winter months. 'Voodoo' is a very vigorous self-branching variety with bold red and aubergine double blooms. 'Marinka' is a truly superb single that will make a beautiful basket very quickly; the upper tube and sepals are bright red, but underneath there's a bell of ruby petals. 'Pink Elephant' is a big, blousy double pink marvel. Huge buds unfurl into layers of soft pink petals. If you love the sound of that, relax and congratulations: you've definitely reached pink-frou-frou nirvana. There are also scores of wonderful doubles and semi-doubles in white and palest pinks, including 'Lauren' and 'Trudi Davro'—blooms that look like mini-bridesmaids that have exploded with vicarious excitement in their uber-flouncy dresses; if you want something in the same appleblossomy shade, more simple yet floriferous, with slightly flared single bell-like flowers, grow 'Time After Time'.

Gaillardia (blanketflower)

HERBACEOUS PERENNIAL OR ANNUAL FOR BORDERS / POTS

Gaillardias are daisies in warm and vibrant bicolour combinations that you may not have grown for quite a long while. It's definitely time to catch up and rediscover them: lots of great breeding work has resulted in new hybrids, mostly perennial *Gaillardia ×grandiflora* types. These newer hybrids are more floriferous and have a sprightly compact habit; they are more tidy and more upright, less floppy than some of the old varieties you may remember. Many make great container and border plants that flower their socks off for months. Propagate by seed or division in spring, root cuttings in autumn. Deadhead regularly; after flowering, trim back, tidy, and feed.

Gaillardia ×grandiflora Mesa is a jolly, early-to-flower series of singles that have split petal tips, giving them a fluttery feel. *Gaillardia* 'Tangerine Spark' is an excellent representative of the new compact hybrids bred for borders and containers; 'Celebration' is a standout fire engine red, and 'Oranges and Lemons' a very popular satsuma sunburst hybrid. Go, Team Gaillardia!

Gaura (beeblossom)

HERBACEOUS PERENNIAL FOR BORDERS / POTS

Gaura lindheimeri is such a pretty, delicate, and unusual plant, I can't imagine my garden without it. Plants have an airy branched structure, with lots of long wiry upright or lax stems carrying masses of flowers. Flowers are either white or pink with four petals and have long elegant stamens. The whole look and feel of the plant in full bloom is a shimmering haze of delicate butterfly-like flowers. Grow from seed or take basal or softwood cuttings in spring, semi-ripe cuttings in summer. Trim back hard after flowering, or treat plants as annuals and grow fresh each year.

The straight species can be tall and rangy, but most of its many selections are more well branched and compact. There's little to distinguish between them: you'll get gorgeous fluttery plants from them all. I love *Gaura lindheimeri* 'Sparkle White'; it's early to flower and very floriferous. There are a number of pink selections, too. My favourites are 'Siskiyou Pink', the upright 'Little Janie', and 'Whiskers Deep Rose', which is among the darkest and sweetly compact.

Gazania

EVERGREEN HERBACEOUS PERENNIAL
FOR BORDERS / POTS

Gazanias are starry, sizzlingly bright South African daisies. They adore hot sunny weather and need a bright open site to do well. The more modern hybrids are better at performing and opening their blooms at lower temperatures and in less than ideal weather. They are tender perennials but are often grown as annuals, and in warm dry gardens they are brilliant planted in huge dazzling drifts as heat- and drought-tolerant groundcover. Propagate by seed (bottom heat) in spring, basal or softwood cuttings in late summer. Plants dislike very heavy or wet soil, so dig in plenty of grit and sand and open it up.

The most vigorous are hybrids, and they tend to be either clumping compact types or spreading. The spreaders are best as groundcovers or trailing over the edge of big terracotta pots. The most dazzling of all are the many boldly striped hybrids, such as 'Giant Bronze Striped' and 'Daybreak XP Rose Stripe'. Indeed, all the stocky F1 hybrids of the Daybreak series are good, with large flowers on short stems and rich green foliage. The pink shades in the Daybreak series change in colour as they mature, so across a group of plants you get a wonderful antique mix of pink and rose tints and tones. The Kiss series of deservedly popular compact F1 hybrids like 'Kiss Mahogany' also includes some large stripy varieties—'Big Kiss White Flame' is the largest-flowering stripy gazania I've seen.

Gerbera

HERBACEOUS PERENNIAL FOR BORDERS / POTS

Gerberas are a globally popular cut flower. It's no surprise that plant breeders have turned their attention to this group of happy, bright, colourful daisies to develop them as plants suitable for bedding out. They have large soft felty flowerheads, or capitulums, which look like a huge single flower, but each head is in fact composed of hundreds of tiny individual flowers. Most cultivars are selections of or hybrids involving *Gerbera jamesonii*. Gerberas come in every colour imaginable apart from true blues, and the length of the flower stems and size of the flowerheads vary greatly: some are as small as 5 cm (2 in.) in diameter, others are closer to 15 cm (6 in.). More versatile and robust varieties are being bred for patios and gardens, but on the whole these are plants that need a good run of warm and dry sunny weather to perform well, and they don't like very wet and damp weather much at all. Grow from seed or plugs. Gerberas struggle with extreme changes, and going quickly from too dry to too wet can be their downfall. Winter wet can be an issue for the hardier types. Keep sheltered in a dry and airy location if you're attempting to overwinter. Garden varieties grow best in consistently moist soil conditions in large containers, or in the ground in warm dry sunny locations.

More and more new types are being introduced to the patio plant market. *Gerbera jamesonii* 'Cartwheel Strawberry Twist' is an award-winning mix of large double-flowered bicolours in pinks, peach, apricot, and creamy yellows. The clear, bold, and rich colours of the EZdazy range are vibrant and full of energy. 'Volcanoes', an orange and yellow bicolour, is impressive. For smaller blooms look for mini-gerberas, robust compact plants often with fully double flowers, where the individual blooms can last a very long time indeed; the Hello! series is a good example.

Helianthus (sunflower)

HERBACEOUS ANNUAL FOR BORDERS / POTS

Sunflowers are both incredibly cheery and easy to grow. The tall and leafy branching giants are great for allotments, cutting gardens, and thin sunny borders next to a fence or wall, where they can be neatly tied in. I find the dwarf and shorter compact varieties more fun to use in displays. They need less room and little to no staking, many are multi-headed, and their attractive seedheads can give a display that lasts well into autumn. Grow from seed; protect young plants from slugs and snails.

The choice of smaller dwarf selections of *Helianthus annuus* has massively increased, and there are now some really unusual and interesting colours. 'Ms Mars' has leaf veins and stems suffused with burgundy, and her petals are the colour of red wine, bleeding out to a pale pinky cream. Short, well branched, and attention-grabbing. 'Teddy Bear' is an adorable double-flowered cuddly lion in rich golden yellow. Being double, the blooms last for weeks. 'Solar Flash' is a great "burning sun" selection, with smouldering burnt orange and yellow bicolour flowers on branched stems. Perfect for containers on the patio. For super-cute and compact, 'Miss Sunshine' is one of the most dwarf and quickest into bloom.

'Inca Gold' is something totally different—a lax, trailing hybrid sunflower with a multi-branching habit and a mass of tiny sunflower blooms, perfect for baskets or as a groundcover.

Helichrysum (liquorice plant)

PERENNIAL FOR BORDERS / POTS / HANGING BASKETS / WINDOW BOXES

Very useful foliage plants—there are silvery grey, golden lime green, and variegated forms, and they all have heart-shaped leaves and a slightly shrubby, spreading to trailing habit. I'm a big fan of soft and felty-leaved *Helichrysum petiolare*; its selection 'Gold' has the most delicate pastel creamy lime or yellow-green foliage colour. *Helichrysum microphyllum* has much smaller dainty foliage; its selection 'Silver Mist' is a slightly more robust and very useful silvery blue plant for beds and containers. Propagate from softwood cuttings. Pinch out plants when young for better branching. Stems can be brittle and break off, so avoid exposed windy spots.

Heliotropium (heliotrope / cherry pie)

PERENNIAL FOR BORDERS / POTS / WINDOW BOXES

Heliotropium arborescens is a most deliciously fragrant thing. Clouds of tiny deep purple, mauve, or white blooms above dark velvety leaves. Be sure to sniff out the highly scented varieties. Their evening scent, emanating from strategically positioned containers on a warm patio or deck, will totally seduce you. Propagate from softwood or semi-hardwood cuttings or seed. Pinch out the tips of young plants for better branching. If you have a bright frost-free place, you can easily overwinter plants.

Seed-raised heliotropes are usually short, compact, and grown as annuals but don't have the strongest scent. Cutting-raised plants of the compact cultivars recommended for strong fragrance are best. The paler types (e.g., *Heliotropium arborescens* 'Nautilus Lavender') can have the strongest scent of all, but visually I love the dark purple ones most, like 'Marino Blue' (another *H. arborescens* selection) and the hybrid 'Dwarf Marine'. Deliciously adorable. *Heliotropium arborescens* 'Lord Roberts' is a classic darker blue-purple with good fragrance; 'Princess Marina' is a slightly lighter mauve-purple and an AGM to boot.

Heuchera / ×Heucherella
(alumroot / coral bells)

EVERGREEN HERBACEOUS PERENNIAL FOR BORDERS / POTS / WINDOW BOXES

As a card-carrying foliage fanatic, I depend more and more on heucheras and heucherellas in my displays. The amount of wonderful cultivars is constantly increasing, and a most exquisite range of plants with dreamy colours within the veins and markings of the leaves is now on offer. Many varieties have an incredible autumnal flush of more intense tones, too. Truly glorious and versatile stocky plants. Many are hardy, so plants can be a great investment, as they're easy to overwinter and can be used year after year. For places where summers are cool and wet and the more tender summer foliage plants like coleus and ipomoeas don't perform, these are a much better bet.

Many of the most popular cultivars are hybrids involving *Heuchera americana*. Those that do well in much hotter sunnier gardens, however, are the often more substantial cultivars of the large and slightly hairy maple-leafed species *H. villosa*—its selection 'Palace Purple' being the prime example. Another group of intergeneric hybrids, crosses of *Heuchera* and *Tiarella*, are given the name ×*Heucherella*. Like heucheras, plants produce rosettes of palmately lobed leaves in a myriad of shades with fine upright delicate panicles of white, green, pink, or red flowers in spring. I fully recommend exploring these adorable and addictive groups of plants. Ideally visit a specialist nursery and shop till you drop. Grow from seed or divide in autumn. Vine weevils and eelworms can be troublesome, particularly when plants are grown in containers in sheltered spots. Treat with nematodes once the weather has warmed up in spring and again in autumn.

Cultivar names for both groups are often very descriptive in terms of their leaf colours. At different times of the year, the leaves of many heuchera hybrids will exhibit different colours and markings, making them even more interesting to grow. 'Marmalade' is a favourite, a wonderful amber to peachy bronze variety that has hot pink undersides to its leaves and frilly edges. If the really dark varieties are your passion, then 'Obsidian' should hit the spot. The metallic-leaved types are incredibly useful, and yet again there are so many excellent varieties; you can have pewter and silver ones like 'Silver Scrolls' or coppery ones like 'September Morn'. 'Carnival Rose Granita' is an incredible metallic silvery pink. Then there is 'Green Spice' and many other lime to acid green chartreuses that are made to make your mouth water.

Some heucheras can suffer from rust disease, but on the whole heucherellas can be more tolerant. I grow 'Tapestry', which has classic green leaves with chocolate brown veining and fluffy candy pink flowers. 'Sweet Tea' is an unusual beige coffee colour with fluffy white flowers.

Hibiscus

HERBACEOUS PERENNIAL OR ANNUAL FOR BORDERS / POTS

There are lots of kinds of hibiscus, but I have two favourite types. The first are the quite new borderline hardy hybrids involving the very big-blooming species *Hibiscus moscheutos*. The dinner-plate-sized blooms are like a fully opened bell, and quite a knockout. They make fine specimen or container plants that pack a huge floral punch. My other favourites are the cultivars of tall *H. acetosella*. They have finely serrated lobed foliage and can add a really unusual and exotic leafy touch. Propagate from seed or hardwood stem cuttings. Plants can overwinter on well-drained soils in sheltered gardens. Cut hard back after frosts have passed, and plants will reshoot from the base. Plants need a very sunny bright spot for the longest period of flower.

For big "tear down those curtains and make me a dress" dramatic blooms, the Luna range (selections of *Hibiscus moscheutos*, of course) has extraordinary flowers that can be up to 18 cm (7 in.) wide. For fancy foliage, you'll want the marvellously tall and elegant hybrid 'Mahogany Splendor', with bronze jagged-edged maple-like leaves, or perhaps the multicoloured *H. acetosella* 'Haight Ashbury', with splashes of cream, pink, and burgundy on deep green-bronze finely serrated foliage—and burgundy flowers in late summer.

Hyacinthus (hyacinth)

PERENNIAL BULB FOR BORDERS / POTS / WINDOW BOXES

Hyacinths (*Hyacinthus orientalis*) are one of my favourite scented bulbs, and so easy to grow. They now come in a really wide range of colours, and those with double blooms seem to last even longer. *Hyacinthus orientalis* 'Woodstock' is a deep beetroot colour, and 'Pink Elephant' is the most gorgeous soft pale pink. 'Eros' is a really unusual double pink selection that has green bracts and a green centre to each flower. Of the many blues I love double 'General Kohler' the most, with its pale powder blue faces and electric blue backs to the petals. 'White Pearl' is one of the purest whites. Grow in good light for best results.

Hydrangea
(hortensia)

DECIDUOUS SHRUB FOR BORDERS /
POTS

Hydrangeas are my favourite flowering shrub, bar none. Recently there has been an explosion in breeding with lots of wonderful new and compact varieties perfect for small gardens and containers. My granddad grew them to perfection, and now I'm loving using them in displays: they help to give real substance and structure to any planting scheme.

There are many species, but my favourites are the big blooming hybrids and selections of *Hydrangea macrophylla* and *H. serrata*, the latter being slightly more hardy, slow growing, and compact. I also totally adore the creamy conical flowerheads of *H. paniculata*, and there are many wonderful new compact cultivars of it, too. Propagate from softwood cuttings. On strongly acidic soils, plants will have bluish flowers, and on alkaline soils, they will be pink, but in containers you can easily control this using a number of products sold specifically to alter the soil pH and thus affect the colour of the blooms. Hydrangeas like consistently moist rich soils to grow well. In late spring, trim back dead, weak, or crossing stems right to the base, and trim back growth to just above the strongest pair of buds to retain a compact plant. Go easy though, as the biggest, fattest, highest buds are the ones that will bloom in summer.

There are two flower types. Mopheads are big, blousy, rounded flowerheads resembling pom-poms, whereas lacecaps have flatter heads with a center of small fertile flowers surrounded by outer rings of showy, sterile bracts. Since flower colour depends on soil pH, an accurate description of the colour of any variety can be a challenge. In my alkaline soil, all my hydrangeas are glorious shades of pink, but even among these, I do have my favourites, each of which brings something slightly different to the party. *Hydrangea macrophylla* 'Swinging Sixties' is a fabulous pink mophead and 'Glam Rock', from the same breeder, is another fun selection—deep pink petals with rich lime green tips that evolve as the blooms mature. *Hydrangea macrophylla* 'Zorro' is a bold and brilliant lacecap with upright stems of a dark beetroot black. 'Little Lime' and 'Baby Lace' are my favourite *H. paniculata* selections—compact plants with cone-shaped panicles that start off entirely lime green. As the sterile florets open, they become paler, eventually turning a creamy white. A slight pink flush gradually strengthens to give a pale pink and creamy lime green mix at maturity.

Iberis (candytuft)

ANNUAL OR PERENNIAL FOR BORDERS / POTS

Soft mini-mounds of four-petalled flowers that are often sweetly scented. *Iberis amara* and *I. umbellata* are hardy annuals; *I. sempervirens* and *I. gibraltarica* are hardy perennials. All are incredibly pretty yet tough as old boots, super-easy to grow, and fast into flower. Plants will take thin poor soils and withstand periods of drought and general neglect and still bloom on all four cylinders. Grow the annual types from seed: rake, sprinkle seed direct, water, you're done. Thin out to allow plants to branch. These will do well pretty much everywhere apart from full shade. More of an alpine plant in some ways. Open, breezy, sunny—they'll love it.

I rather love the pale pastel mauves and pinks and the darker colours. They all look wonderful amongst silvery grey foliage plants. *Iberis gibraltarica* is a free-flowering mauve and white that's a pure delight, and 'Pink Ice' is a lovely large-flowered, blushing lilac pink hybrid concoction. Most often you'll see the bright, uncompromisingly icy white varieties. For a bomb-proof perennial with flattish umbel-like flowers, grow *Iberis sempervirens* 'Whiteout'.

Impatiens

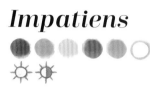

PERENNIAL FOR BORDERS / POTS / WINDOW BOXES

Impatiens walleriana (busy lizzie) hybrids, with their succulent fleshy stems, gentle apple green foliage, and endless bright cheery blooms, were one of the most popular and versatile plants for bedding out through the summer. Plants grow and flower well in sun but are brilliant at providing colour in very shady locations. Then in the early noughties, downy mildew became a huge problem for growers and gardeners alike, and many of us stopped growing them. In the meantime the larger more showy and substantial hybrids of *I. hawkeri* (New Guinea impatiens) that are naturally resistant to mildew have become a little more popular. They prefer warmer and brighter locations, so aren't quite as versatile but are glamorous plants to grow, delivering what I like to call "electric landlady" pinks and purples quite unlike any other flower. New breeding programmes between the two types have yielded bold and brilliant mildew-resistant interspecific hybrids that will tolerate semi-shady sites. Propagate from seed or softwood cuttings. They can be tricky plants to grow from seed, but stem-tip cuttings root quickly and easily. Overwinter your favourites as houseplants in a bright window bottom.

For incredible Day-Glo disco colours (which I have a freaky fondness for), grow the Color-Power series. You'll need big sunglasses for these eye-poppingly bright selections of *Impatiens hawkeri*.

The mildew-resistant hybrids of the Divine series have really large blooms and come in a gorgeously rich range of colours. Some have glossy bronze leaves, too. This series will tolerate short spells of wet damp weather. 'Divine Violet' is a stunning rich magenta.

Big Bounce is a new series of interspecific impatiens with a gentle mounding habit. Plants bounce back quickly when they have suffered a dry spell, tolerate partial shade, and have good downy mildew resistance.

Ipomoea
(morning glory / sweet potato)

PERENNIAL OR ANNUAL FOR BORDERS / POTS /
HANGING BASKETS / WINDOW BOXES

Ipomoeas are brilliantly useful plants for bedding displays, and for me they fall into two groups. The first are the wiry twining vines grown for their wide, frequently blue or purple floral trumpets, reminiscent of a gramophone's horn, and often treated as annual climbers, although many are in fact tender perennials. However, the unusual *Ipomoea lobata* (Spanish flag) is for me the most wonderful and easy of these tender climbers. It has racemes of small tubular flowers and twining stems flushed reddish bronze which scramble over trellises, fences, and wigwams. The individual flowers begin bright tangerine red, and as they mature down the inflorescence they turn orange, yellow, and creamy white. It will do well in slightly cooler spots, where some of the other climbing types can struggle.

Then there's the spreading and trailing *Ipomoea batatas* (sweet potato) types, grown for their lush and colourful heart-shaped and finger-like lobed leaves. They're a favourite foliage plant of mine but need a warm sunny summer to thrive. Propagate from seed (bottom heat) or softwood cuttings. Soak the seeds of climbing types overnight in lukewarm water, and sow individually in pots in moist rich soil. Stem cuttings of ornamental sweet potato types will root quickly. All ipomoeas need constant warm temperatures to do well.

The Bright Ideas and Sweet Caroline series offer lush well-branched selections of *Ipomoea batatas* in lime greens, blacks, and bronze reds; Sweet Caroline Sweetheart selections have slightly smaller, more (you guessed it) heart-shaped leaves. Illusion selections have fine finger-like lobed leaves that give a lacy feel to the plant; 'Illusion Midnight Lace' is a deeply divided jet black jewel, and 'Illusion Garnet Lace' has lime green leaves when small and young, but they turn coffee-olive-bronze as they mature. Just gorgeous. *Ipomoea batatas* 'Suntory Black Tone' is a good matte black.

Iresine (bloodleaf)

PERENNIAL FOR BORDERS / POTS

The bloodleafs are a total knockout, with some of the most vibrant foliage you'll ever encounter. These shrubby, tender, tropical-heat- and moisture-loving plants can add a colourful and exotic edge, and I rather love them. Best of all are the crazy pink leaves of *Iresine herbstii* (beefsteak plant); and my favourite selection of that favourite species is 'Red Heart', which is a wonderfully wild electric cherry red-pink. Propagate from softwood cuttings. Use a dilute balanced feed to encourage good leaf colour.

Isotoma (star flower / laurentia)

PERENNIAL FOR POTS / HANGING BASKETS / WINDOW BOXES

Isotoma axillaris is a pretty Australian relative of *Lobelia*. It's floriferous and vigorous yet elegant and refined, and I've really come to love growing it or its cultivars (e.g., 'Avant-garde Pink', 'Blue Star', 'Indigo Stars') on their own in containers. The delicately scented star-shaped blooms, in pale powdery pastel pinks, lilacs, mauves, and whites, shoot out on long thin stems from lacy green foliage, forming wonderfully dense mounds. Plants thrive in containers and baskets in rich soil in a warm bright airy location. Best treated as an annual and grown from softwood cuttings or plugs.

Jacobaea
(silver ragwort / dusty miller)

EVERGREEN PERENNIAL FOR BORDERS / POTS / WINDOW BOXES

I'm rather fond of *Jacobaea maritima*, a silvery grey foliage plant used in traditional bedding schemes. It has undergone several nomenclatural changes, so you may still find it as *Senecio cineraria* or *Cineraria maritima*. Various forms of dusty miller are available, from those with very divided filigree leaves to super-felty scallop-edged types. It's a shrubby perennial plant best kept fresh and grown as an annual from seed. Plants will tolerate slight shade but do best in full sun. Cut any flowering stems hard back to encourage lush leafy growth. 'Silver Dust' is the classic finely divided selection, but my favourite for fully tomentose wavy-edged woolly foliage is the broader-leaved 'Cirrus'.

Lantana (yellow sage)

EVERGREEN PERENNIAL FOR BORDERS / POTS / HANGING BASKETS / WINDOW BOXES

Lantana camara and its cultivars are delicious things. Whether upright or trailing, you get quite a shrubby plant packed with clustered globes of tiny honey-scented blooms that specialise in colour transformations. The individual florets usually turn from pale delicate colours into deeper more intense shades. The leaves are the texture of fine sandpaper and often have an aromatic citrus or pineapple-like scent. Butterflies and hummingbirds adore these plants, and the rainbow range of available varieties is a full-on floral Mardi Gras. Fun plants for warm sunny spots or conservatories. Grow from seed or semi-hardwood cuttings. Keep plants well fed with a high-potassium fertiliser to encourage blooms. These are great heat-tolerant plants once established; in fact, they relish and flower better in very hot sunny weather.

The Luscious series is a collection of versatile and floriferous medium-height mounding selections good for baskets as well as borders and containers. *Lantana camara* 'Luscious Marmalade' is a rich orange, and 'Luscious Pinkberry Blend' a candy pink and primrose mixture. The Lucky and Tiddley Winks hybrid series are likewise floriferous; the first offers tight compact plants, and those in the well-branched Tiddley Winks range will gently trail over the edge of containers.

Lavandula (lavender)

☀

EVERGREEN PERENNIAL FOR BORDERS / POTS /
WINDOW BOXES

There are almost forty species of lavenders, and many cultivars of *Lavandula angustifolia* are used as culinary herbs and grown especially for their wonderful fragrance. I adore hardy angustifolias, but for bedding out and container displays I love the more showy flowers of *L. stoechas* (French lavender), with their bunny-ear petals (flags), and also some of the more unusual species, like *L. pedunculata* and *L. multifida*, which are perfect for pots. These are tough heat- and drought-tolerant plants once established, but they need a sunny open spot and shelter from wet and cold to get through hard winters. Propagate from softwood or semi-ripe cuttings. Lavenders hate very wet or heavy soils, so mix in plenty of grit and ensure drainage is good.

Lavandula stoechas 'Bandera Purple' is compact and mounding; it has black-purple flowerheads with purple flags. *Lavandula pedunculata* subsp. *pedunculata* 'James Compton', an AGM, has large rich purple flowerheads with tall pale mauve ribbon-like tufts. *Lavandula pedunculata* subsp. *sampaiana* 'Purple Emperor' is a tall, dark, handsome devil with violet flowerheads and rich plum burgundy ears. *Lavandula multifida* 'Spanish Eyes' is a gorgeous ferny-leaved lavender that's fast to grow and free flowering with lots of airy spikes of mauve flowers. Slightly more tender but wonderful.

Lavatera

☀

ANNUAL FOR BORDERS / POTS

Lavatera belongs to the marvellous mallow plant family, which includes hollyhocks and hibiscus. The huge satin funnels of *L. trimestris* (annual mallow) and its selections come in pinks and whites. The Twins series has short and floriferous selections in hot pink and pure white, and the award-winning Beauty series offers compact upright plants with shallowly lobed rounded foliage and large flowers in pinks and whites, some with dark veining. In terms of flower power, annual mallows are hard to beat, and they make substantial plants that are easy to grow from seed. Plants don't like root disturbance, so ideally direct sow or grow them individually in 9 cm (3.5 in.) pots. Space them out to encourage well-branched stocky plants.

Lobelia

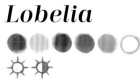

PERENNIAL OR ANNUAL FOR BORDERS /
POTS / HANGING BASKETS /
WINDOW BOXES

Lobelia erinus is the undeniably dainty blue and white bedding plant traditionally used to edge beds and borders and seen tumbling out of hanging baskets. The lobelias derived from it are either neat compact upright forms or looser trailing types. Many of the classic upright seed-raised selections have been improved over the years, but on the whole, the vigorous cutting-raised cultivars that are now available have more impact: plants are more robust and longer flowering, with slightly bigger blooms.

Lobelia erinus is just one of many species lobelias that are now popular as patio plants and ornamentals for bedding out. There's *L. cardinalis* (cardinal flower) and its cultivars, with wonderful spires in reds and purples, and also tall herbaceous upright blues like *L. valida*. Grow from seed or cuttings. Mix the tiny seed of *L. erinus* with horticultural sand to make sowing easier. Trim back plants after flowering, and feed plants to promote a new flush of flowers. Most lobelias like a more moisture- and nutrient-rich soil than they're often planted in. The dainty blooms can struggle in hot sun and drying winds, so sheltered places with dappled light are better.

Among traditional bedding lobelias are upright seed-raised classics like *Lobelia erinus* 'Crystal Palace' (deep blue flowers and bronze foliage) and 'Mrs Clibran' (white blotch on inky blue flowers and green foliage); both are AGMs. There are scores of seed-raised trailing and semi-trailing types; I prefer those in the later-flowering Fountain series, such as *L. erinus* 'Fountain Lilac'. My favourite range of cutting-raised bedding lobelias is the Waterfall series; *L. erinus* 'Waterfall Blue', with large rich blue flowers, is yet another AGM. But the Laguna and Lucia ranges of hybrids are said to have better heat tolerance for hotter gardens.

I prefer to plant taller upright herbaceous lobelias in borders and to add height in containers. *Lobelia valida* 'Delft Blue' is a compact floriferous plant with stunning sky blue flowers with a white eye that are held in upright spires. The slightly succulent foliage is a light fresh green. *Lobelia ×speciosa* 'Starship Scarlet', a knockout lipstick red, challenges the classic *L. cardinalis* 'Queen Victoria'.

Lupinus (lupin)

HERBACEOUS PERENNIAL OR ANNUAL FOR BORDERS / POTS

Lupins are fun to grow for bedding out. The blue annual species from seed are stunning, the shorter bedding hybrids have their own special sweet charm, and the huge range of bigger perennial cultivars can be used if you really want to up the impact, height, and size of bloom. Plants are best sown direct; nick or chip the seed and soak overnight before sowing. Otherwise, sow early in spring under glass in 9 cm (3.5 in.) pots.

Lupins offered as seed that make shortish plants for a display are often hybrids involving a wide range of species. The dwarf Gallery series holds short stocky hybrids in a good range of colours, and the *Lupinus hartwegii* Avalune series is also excellent. But I must admit I've come to love the intense blue you get from annuals—like *L. mutabilis* 'Sunrise' and bluest of all *L. subcarnosus* and *L. texensis*, the Texas bluebonnets—the most.

Muscari (grape hyacinth)

PERENNIAL BULB FOR BORDERS / POTS / WINDOW BOXES

I've always loved the dense spikes of tiny urn-shaped flowers that make up the mini "bunch of grapes" blooms of muscari in spring. These are tough and adorable little bulbs, and they come in a wide range of different blues as well as in white and pale pink. In some cultivars the upper flowers are a different colour and shape to the lower ones. These really easy-to-grow bulbs add a fun flower form to spring displays; they will multiply quickly if planted in good free-draining soil, and some will seed themselves liberally, too, so deadhead to prevent an invasion.

For extra fragrance grow the sweetly scented rich blue *Muscari armeniacum*, *M. botryoides* 'Album', and the wonderfully unusual *M. macrocarpum* 'Golden Fragrance', which is acid yellow topped with plum purple. I get rather giddy for the pale and powdery blue types; *M. azureum*, *M. armeniacum* 'Valerie Finnis', and the hybrid 'Jenny Robinson' are all favourites. *Muscari latifolium* is rather special—mostly blue-black flowers with a top hat of sterile blue-violet ones—whereas 'Mount Hood', a hybrid, has frosted ice white florets capping vivid flowers of aqua blue. 'Pink Sunrise', another hybrid, is an achingly lovely soft pale rose. *Muscari aucheri* 'White Magic' is a fresh lime yellow in bud, opening to pure white.

Myosotis
(forget-me-not)

HERBACEOUS BIENNIAL FOR BORDERS /
POTS / WINDOW BOXES

It's hard to imagine spring bedding without this most dainty and archetypal flower. Spring hasn't fully sprung unless there's some sort of forget-me-not frothiness going on in my garden. The traditional tiny baby blue flowers are totally gorgeous and hard to beat amongst biennials and bulbs. More recently I've been experimenting with white and pink forms, which are fun to use, too. Some are hybrids involving the shorter alpine species *Myosotis alpestris* and the taller woodland species *M. sylvatica*. Grow from seed. The only downfall is mildew. Keep an organic baking soda–based mildew drench at the ready. Forget-me-nots can self-seed profusely, so have a trowel to dig up seedlings to grow on for next year's display. For full-on frothiness, the slightly taller looser types are better.

The Sylva series offers reliably good selections of *Myosotis sylvatica*; 'Rosylva' is my current pink obsession. Amongst short plants and dwarf bulbs grow 'Mon Amie Blue' or 'Victoria Blue', and for tall pure blue daintiness grow 'Royal Blue Improved', all selections of *M. sylvatica*.

Narcissus *(daffodil)*

PERENNIAL BULB FOR BORDERS / POTS / WINDOW BOXES

Narcissi are such wonderful and easy plants to grow. The shorter, smaller-flowered, and highly scented types are my favourites, with their nodding noses and swept-back petals. These are brilliant bulbs for containers and small gardens, and they're a flower I never tire of—you can never have too many. Plant three times as deep as the bulb, pointy end facing upwards. Feed and lightly water as they begin to flower. Deadhead and leave the foliage for six weeks to build up the bulb for next year.

'Tête-à-tête' is the hugely popular, very low-growing golden dwarf daffodil that's totally cute. My list of favourite short rich yellows, which are perhaps even more lovely, includes 'Peeping Tom', 'Jumblie', and 'Quail'. I love the more acid to lemon yellows, too; 'Hawera' is a short slender triandrus type you'll totally fall in love with. For hot tangerine-orange trumpets and eggy yellow petals, you must have 'Jetfire' and 'Katherine Jenkins'.

My latest obsession is varieties with lemon, white, and cream colouring. They can give a gentle pale primrose, buttercream, or soft citrus tint to a display. 'Thalia', 'Ice Wings', 'Petrel', and 'Verona' are all elegant, spellbinding whites. 'Segovia', 'Dutch Lemon Drops', 'Jack Snipe', and 'Topolino' are all soft yet slightly sherbety. For pale creamy heavily scented double blooms, grow 'Bridal Crown', 'Sir Winston Churchill', and 'Cheerfulness'. The creamy yellow version of the latter, 'Yellow Cheerfulness', is pure primrose-scented goodness, but my ultimate heavenly scented variety is 'Geranium' with its clusters of fragrant creamy flowers with deep orangey central cups.

'Green Eyed Lady' and 'Green Pearl' are unusual daffodils with a slightly green eye or lime green freshness about them, respectively. If you adore teeny-tiny-flowered daffodils on grassy elegant stems, grow 'Baby Boomer' and 'Pipit'. Finally for taller, more substantial frou-frou peachy and creamy whites, try 'Kaydee', 'Delnashaugh', and 'Exotic Beauty', which is totally ooo-la-la.

Nemesia

HERBACEOUS PERENNIAL OR ANNUAL FOR BORDERS / POTS / HANGING BASKETS / WINDOW BOXES

Nemesias are a jaunty and colourful group of plants that have flowers with an upper petal consisting of four lobes and the lower petal of two. Traditionally the quite frilly and large-flowered South African species *Nemesia strumosa* was the most popular for bedding, and it and its upright but slightly floppy-flowered offspring remain my favourites. Strumosas are easy from seed and often have a large central eye with attractive markings. The bushy *N. fruticans* and its cultivars have smaller flowers but tend to be more branched and free flowering, with slightly more rigid, erect stems and a gentle pleasant fragrance, too. There's something slightly retro and '70s about them that I love. There are, however, lots of different species and cultivars that can be used in displays, from hardier perennial types to more tender ones often grown as annuals, and recent breeding work has yielded all sorts of hybrids with different growth habits, floriferousness, and flower forms, a bigger range of colours, and often longer flowering periods, too. Grow from seed or softwood cuttings. In very hot dry locations, flowering can shut down. Keep plants well fed and watered, and trim back straight after flowering to encourage a second flush.

Nemesia strumosa 'Fire King' is a rich single devil-red selection, and 'White Knight' is one to grow for cutting for pure white wedding flowers. 'Sundrops' is a well-branched strumosa hybrid which has particularly large flowers in strong punchy colours with a rich eye; 'Tapestry' is a painterly mix of unusually coloured flowers that have gorgeous markings, whereas 'Carnival Mix' offers brilliant brights, tints, and tones.

Among the fruticans types, Poetry is a series of seed-raised hybrids that give the cutting-raised types a good run for their money. Aromatica is a series of scented hybrids that cope well in warmer temperatures. 'Innocence', a hardy white AGM, has been involved in the breeding of several other hybrids; there's 'Compact Innocence', 'Refined Innocence', 'Pink Innocence', and 'Opal Innocence'—and probably many more on their way. The Lady series offers bicolours in gentle pale pastels that are highly fragrant, beautifully feminine, and have the classic tiny yellow lips at their centres. For clear colours with little to no yellow Tweetie-Pie lips at their centre, look to the sweetly scented Lagoon series.

Blue and purple nemesias can be a good alternative to using lobelias in displays; *Nemesia fruticans* 'Blue Lagoon' is a standout, as are the hybrids 'Poetry Blue' and 'KLM', which is a blue and white bicolour (and slightly more strumosa-like).

The French Connection is a delicious series; 'Myrtille' is an inky indigo-purple hybrid with a magenta lip, and 'Framboise' a raspberry that fades to antique rose.

Finally, Juicy Fruits and Sunsatia nemesias are the perfect marriage of the old-fashioned strumosas and the more modern fruticans. Incredibly bushy, robust, and floriferous plants, in eye-popping single hues to stunningly marked bi- and tricolours to the subtlest sugary and fruity pastels. Tasty and tasteful rainbow ranges that really have it all. I want to revel in them.

Nicotiana (tobacco plant)

HERBACEOUS ANNUAL FOR BORDERS / POTS

Nicotianas are a favourite fragrant summer bedding plant, and I like to grow a lot of them. They're also one of the very best lime green–flowered plants in the garden, so that's two massive big ticks on the flower-powered checklist of "good to have." The shorter varieties often have more upward-facing tubular star-faced flowers, but although they're super-floriferous they aren't nearly as scented as some of the taller types. Visually I'm rather taken with the very tall ones with long tubular white flowers and also what I call mutable varieties. On a warm summer evening a garden with lots of fragrant nicotianas is heady and heavenly. Grow from seed (bottom heat). Sow seed on the surface in gentle warmth and keep gently moist. Plants are beloved by slugs and snails, so protect when planting out.

If you're going to have a display involving nicotianas, it seems criminal to miss out on their fragrance. Medium-height series like Perfume and Eau de Cologne are my favourites and come in a great range of colours. For tall, white, and scented, try *Nicotiana suaveolens* and *N. ×sanderae* 'Fragrant Cloud'—great fragrance. *Nicotiana sylvestris*, a tassled, big-leaved, long-tubed wonder, is hugely rewarding to grow, but you do need lots of room for it. *Nicotiana alata* 'Grandiflora' has possibly the most powerful perfume of all.

The medium to tall hybrid 'Whisper Mixed' has mutable flowers that start off white and turn through ever-deepening shades of pink. Bushy, floriferous, and very faintly scented. *Nicotiana* 'Lime Green' is a superb (AGM) medium-height lime green. *Nicotiana langsdorffii* will bring more green and a dash of delightful curiosity to any display; it has panicles of small dangling acid green flowers with bizarre blue pollen. Diddly little floral hats that belong to the absinthe fairy.

Ocimum (basil)

HERBACEOUS ANNUAL FOR BORDERS / POTS

Most culinary and ornamental basils are selections of *Ocimum basilicum*, some with extraordinary leaf colours: 'Cinnamon' has bronzy emerald leaves with a spicy scent (and gorgeous pink flowers); the leaves of 'Dark Opal', 'Purple Ball', and var. *purpurascens* 'Purple Ruffles' are a brilliant deep plum purple; the big bright green, crinkled leaves of 'Green Ruffles' have a mild aniseed taste. Grow from seed. Plants love to be warm, moist, and sheltered from strong winds.

Osteospermum
(African daisy)

HERBACEOUS PERENNIAL FOR BORDERS / POTS / HANGING BASKETS / WINDOW BOXES

Osteospermums are floriferous sun-loving daisies that it's hard not to like. They're available in a myriad of refreshing, fashionable, and now even more bold and subtle new colours. The latest hybrids are often very compact plants, brilliant for containers, and often best grown as annuals. The vigorous evergreen semi-hardy perennial types are great at the front of large borders or as groundcovers. When they do their jazzy floral razzle-dazzle, I'm dancing along with them. Grow from seed or softwood cuttings. Moderately rich but very sharply draining soil and an open sunny site is required for a really good display.

From seed, the F1 hybrids of the Akila series are well-branched compact plants in whites, purples, and mauves, but I'm really taken with all the unusual new colours. The Serenity series is a great example. 'Serenity Bronze' has orangey bronze petals that bleed into neon pink as they reach the magenta purple eye. 'Serenity Lemonade' is a fresh citrus yellow. Those in the Magic series change colour as the flowers mature to give a subtle blended range of tints and tones of peach, apricot, and rose. Wonderful and unusual. For a more lax loose trailing habit, the sunny Sunbrella series has floriferous large-petalled hybrids in rich and creamy pastel tones.

A favourite vigorous cream variety of mine is 'Voltage White'. Soft white petals and a pale primrose-coloured middle. 'Voltage Yellow' is an outstandingly dazzling canary yellow. Both hybrids are totally floriferous and hard to beat en masse in borders.

The 3D series of anemone-centred hybrids is rather special. Plants have a very tight neat habit. The colour range is white, cream, yellows, mauves, and rich purples. Perfect plants for small pots on patios and balconies and because of their form, the flowers will stay open whatever the weather. Daisies that sing even in the rain.

Pelargonium
(geranium / storksbill)

HERBACEOUS PERENNIAL FOR
BORDERS / POTS / HANGING BASKETS /
WINDOW BOXES

All bedding geraniums, botanically speaking, are pelargoniums. The genus contains in excess of two hundred species, but most of the commonly cultivated plants are complex hybrids that have *Pelargonium zonale* somewhere in their heritage. My granddad's favourites were the blousy-bloomed and serrate-leaved regal pelargoniums, which now, like him, I adore too. In terms of a hard-working, floriferous, and utterly brilliant group of plants for bedding out, pelargoniums are very hard to beat. Not only are they available in the most incredible range of colours and flower forms, but this group has the added advantage of types grown for wonderfully scented, textured, and variegated foliage and naturally trailing and cascading types, too. They are also one of the easiest tender plants to keep from one year to the next on a bright frost-free window bottom indoors. There are many distinct groups of pelargoniums, and most will work well in bedding and container displays. Many of the types sold as bedding varieties are robust and utterly brilliant, but let these just be the start to your exploration of this amazingly diverse set of extraordinary plants. Propagate from seed (bottom heat) or softwood cuttings. The range available to grow from seed is relatively small, but specialist nurseries will have an incredible range of choice varieties, often offered as rooted cuttings in plugs or young plants. Give plants a high-potassium feed during the growing season and deadhead regularly. Plants will survive the winter in a semi-dormant state if kept dry, cool, and frost-free.

Zonal pelargoniums. These are the widely grown, archetypal "bedding geraniums." Singles have five petals per floret, and all cluster together to form big flowerheads that are either quite tight or loose, depending on the variety. Double and semi-double zonals are more popular, with more petals giving a much fuller flowerhead. They also last longer than the flowers of the single forms.

My favourite seed-raised zonals instantly tick two boxes, for flower and foliage interest, as they have very dark leaf zoning. The F1 Bullseye series comes in a great range of colours with bold chocolate felty foliage. For a robust range of different colours, the F1 Horizon series is hard to beat. There are some interesting picotee and "ice" types, where the individual petals are pale in the centre and highlighted by a dark petal edge; the ripple types are fun, too, if you're open to something a bit different or have a total weakness for flowers that evoke raspberry ripple ice cream. Among cutting-raised zonals, the Fantasia series holds bold varieties with dark foliage in a good range of colours.

Interspecific hybrids between zonal and ivy leaf pelargoniums are new on the scene. The resulting plants can have either a more upright habit or be more trailing. The Boldly series of five lush rich colours (and counting) raises the bar for super-robust bedding-style plants that are, like zonals, upright in habit. The five offerings in the Timeless range are more trailing and ivy-leaved.

Ivy leaf / trailing pelargoniums. Cultivars of *Pelargonium peltatum* have glossy, almost succulent leaves and a trailing habit. Balcony types (e.g., the astoundingly floriferous Decora and Cascade series) have masses of thin-petalled single-flowered trusses. There are also semi- and fully double-flowered types with heavy opulent heads of blooms; charming swirly-petalled rosebud types (e.g., the widely available and rather gorgeous Sybil series); and some variegated and unusual leaf types ('Evka', with carmine pink flowers and silver, green, and white variegated leaves, is outstanding). Perfect for baskets, window boxes, planting pouches, Woolly Pockets—anywhere they can hang out. Very drought tolerant and will keep flowering until the first hard frost.

Relatively few ivy leaf pelargoniums are available from seed. The best cutting-raised ivy leaf varieties branch well and have short internodes and great floral impact. The Precision series offers good strong well-branched plants in a great range of shades. 'Tommy' is my favourite rich claret wine double; its long flower stems work well when growing amongst other plants in pouches and baskets. 'Spanish Burgundy Wine' is another slightly more compact variety I also adore. There are some great bicolours, too: 'Rouletta' is a cherry red and white, and 'Harlequin Rosie O'Day' a candy pink and white. 'Surcouf' is an old classic with single red-violet blooms.

Fancy-leaved pelargoniums. I love the classic tricolour types. 'Mrs Pollock' and 'Skies of Italy' have green and golden variegated leaves and red-orange flowers, but 'Pink Dolly Varden' with blushing pink blooms and cream variegation is my favourite. 'Frank Headley' is a classic silver and green variegated cultivar with shrimp pink flowers, and 'Mrs Parker' is similar but with deeper rose pink blooms. Plants in the Pelgardini series are produced from "cleaned" disease-free stock; virus and disease buildup can be an issue with some of the older Victorian varieties.

Scented-leaved pelargoniums. Varieties like 'Lady Plymouth' are worth growing for their strongly scented citrusy leaves alone. Those with a good balance of both flower and foliage, however, are doubly good. 'Pink Capitatum' is a favourite—good big fluffy pink flowers and apple green crinkled foliage with the yummy scent of a fruit salad. 'Attar of Roses' is similar but with a wonderful rose scent. 'Orange Fizz' has strongly citrus-scented foliage and also good "angel" type flowers, where the top two petals have deep burgundy blotches that contrast with the pale lilac mauve of the rest of the bloom. The handsome and compact 'Royal Oak' has deep green oak-shaped leaves with a central chocolatey blotch and a pleasant balsam scent, as well as pretty mauve flowers. If you want cedar-scented leaves, go for 'Clorinda', as it also has gorgeous big rich rose pink blooms. Finally 'Deerwood Lavender Lad' not only has a unique lavender fragrance but little magenta fairy-like flowers.

Unique pelargoniums. This is a group of scented types that have much bigger, more impressive, more colourful flowers. 'Voodoo' is a standout—dark velvety devil-red and maroon flowers; 'Mystery' is similarly wicked. Both are AGMs. If you're drawn to shockingly bright varieties, try 'Rollison's Unique', 'Scarlet Unique', and 'Claret Rock Unique', which are zingy colours from bright magenta pink to a sort of electric disco red. For a gentle pastel pink with the most exquisite and delicate magenta purple veining, grow 'Madame Auguste Nonin'.

Regal pelargoniums. These are the types my granddad would grow to show standards. I love their serrated zigzag-edged leaves and their large azalea-like flowers. Regals are easy to grow, early to flower, floriferous, and super-flouncy. The Aristo series is a good starting point; its plants are compact and come in a great range of colours. 'Turkish Coffee' is a very unusual and tempting caramel pink. 'Kaufman's Bonfire' is a wonder, billed as a "purple-pink over scarlet, blazed purple." I'd describe the petal colour as a fight between hot lipstick pink and raspberry sauce. Outrageous and addictive.

'Dark Secret' is one of the largest and most solid clear dark burgundies, but the battle for "blackest" rages between 'Venus' and 'Aristo Schoko'. All three belong to the dark side. 'Lord Bute' is also a Sith Lord of sorts with petals like velvety deep crimson cloaks, each with a menacing margin of lightsabre-bright scarlet.

In total contrast I love the pink and white super-frilly varieties. Try 'Parisienne', 'Fleur d'Amour', 'Rosmaroy', 'Joan Morf', 'Delli', and 'Birthday Girl'. All a candy-floss sugar rush. The most Moulin Rouge cancan girl of the lot is 'The Marchioness of Bute'. Black cherry, white, and crimson rippled crimped petals with bright glowing margins. Pure high kicks and ooh la la.

Rosebuds. These pelargoniums have rounded fully double tightly packed individual blooms and are really good fun. 'Apple Blossom Rosebud' is a gorgeous pink and white bicolour with big floppy green leaves. 'Australian Pink Rambler' can become a huge shrubby plant and has gorgeous rich candy pink blooms. More compact varieties in good shades of pink include 'Wedding Royale', 'Sweet Jess', and 'Noele Gordon'.

Pennisetum
(ornamental millet / fountain grass)

● ● ● ●

☼

HERBACEOUS PERENNIAL GRASS FOR
BORDERS / POTS

Pennisetums stand out as one of the most
graceful grasses to include in container and
bedding displays; their large fluffy flower
plumes, which often change colour as they
mature, are pure elegance. Incorporate
them to add movement and texture and
make any display feel lighter, fresher, and
more contemporary, too. The pennisetums that work best in mixed container
plantings are often more open and airy,
with the most colourful and impressive
foxtail flower plumes. *Pennisetum ×advena*
'Rubrum' is one of the most popular. Dark
red foliage that's initially flushed green
emerges in spring. The arching stems have
fluffy silver bottlebrush-like plumes in late
summer to autumn, turning red and then chestnut brown. The robust and solid-looking
cultivars of *P. purpureum* (elephant grass) and *P. glaucum* (African millet) are brilliant in
leafy subtropical-style plantings and for adding a bit of sophisticated stateliness to a more
structured scheme. *Pennisetum purpureum* contributes wide leaf blades with lots of impact;
'Prince' and 'Princess' are robust selections with strong burgundy and purple colours in the
foliage. *Pennisetum glaucum* 'Jade Princess' is a gorgeous short selection with bright apple
green leaves and stocky brick red plumes; the green and burgundy 'Purple Baron' and the
much darker and taller 'Purple Majesty' are two of the most popular glaucum selections and
my favourites. Plants can be green at first but turn darker as they mature in the sun. Propagate by division or seed (bottom heat). Plants like quite rich but very sharply draining soils
and sunny airy locations.

Penstemon (beardtongue)

☀

HERBACEOUS PERENNIAL FOR BORDERS / POTS

Penstemons are fun and easy plants to propagate from seed or cuttings (softwood or semi-ripe). Their spires of tubular blooms are showy and brightly hued, and many of the most colourful cultivars lend themselves to temporary displays, as they have a half-hardy nature. I enjoy them, and they can feel like a slightly more modern choice for temporary summer displays with a mix of plants like grasses and echinaceas. Resist tidying up plants until spring. Some will overwinter well in sheltered spots. To keep plants compact and self-supporting, trim back to lowest shoots once frosts have passed. Take summer cuttings and bring on new plants.

Blue cultivars are popular, as always. My favourites are 'Electric Blue' and 'Heavenly Blue' (both selections of *Penstemon heterophyllus*) and the hybrids 'Blue Riding Hood' and 'Jean Grace'. Unusual plants that have slightly greyish green foliage and bright blue flowers that often turn lilac and mauve as they age.

Penstemon barbatus 'Cambridge Mixed', readily available as seed, offers compact plants with greyish green foliage that are fast into flower in a good range of pinks and mauves. Tubular Bells and Sea series are more dwarf hybrids with good basal branching. Pensham is a wonderful award-winning series bred by Edward Wilson in the United Kingdom. There's an incredible range of colours, and they're hard to beat. My favourite, 'Pensham Just Jayne', has magenta and rose pink flowers borne continuously on tall spikes well into autumn.

Perilla

☀

HERBACEOUS ANNUAL FOR BORDERS / POTS / WINDOW BOXES

Perilla frutescens (shiso) is the aromatic leafy herb popular in Asian cuisine. It's a really useful plant for adding leafy texture and colour to displays, and there are all sorts of wonderful red-, purple-, and green-leaved forms. Its attractive zigzaggedy-edged leaves look slightly like those of stinging nettle. Darker leaf forms make the perfect foil for all sorts of bedding flowers in rich bright hues. *Perilla frutescens* var. *crispa* and *P. frutescens* var. *purpurascens* are, respectively, the super-crinkly-edged and popular deep purple shisos that I grow from seed.

Petunia

HERBACEOUS PERENNIAL FOR BORDERS / POTS / HANGING
BASKETS / WINDOW BOXES

Forget all your preconceptions. If ever there was a group of plants
that deserves another look, a really fresh start, it's petunias without
a doubt. Some of the new colours and novelties are absolutely fabulous. Edina and Patsy would approve. Every colour imaginable apart
from a true blue, all sorts of extraordinary bicolours and blends, and
rims, stripes, and speckles artistically splattered on and over everything from huge grandiflora-sized blooms to much smaller milliflora
types. I revel in them. I've always loved them, even the huge floppy
ones that used to struggle in wet and windy weather. Lots of great
breeding work in recent years means that the new modern varieties
are massive improvements over their forebears. Petals are sturdier, and the blooms of some
have a quasi-funnelled star shape to help rain trickle away. There are more mounding varieties better suited to beds and borders and semi- and fully trailing types, too. All are tender
perennials best grown as annuals. Grow from seed or softwood cuttings. Slugs love them, so
get protection in place as soon as you plant out. Deadhead regularly.

Singles. Surfinia is possibly the best-known series of all modern hybrid petunias. These
have a trailing habit and medium to large single flowers in a truly incredible range
of colours. I adore the veined types in particular. Similar to them are the Wave series.
Easy Wave is quick to flower, mounding and spreading with no pinching out required.
Petunia ×atkinsiana Tidal Wave holds the most vigorous plants I've encountered; these will
scale walls and trellises if planted closely together, very much like an advancing tsunami
of flowers.

The Supertunia and Vista series are vigorous and robust, so perfect for covering large areas
with carpets of flowers and also spilling out from big containers; 'Vista Silverberry' has a
stunning deep pink centre that bleeds gently into palest pink petals. Express and Fanfare
are yet more popular series. These flower early and have big gorgeous grandiflora single
blooms and a trailing habit. Hard to fault them.

Doubles. Double petunias will always be gloriously over-the-top. That's their job,
and I adore them for it. They bloom like a group of tipsy cancan girls having a full-on
knicker-flashing moment. I adore the Superbissima series for its selection of big delicious
frilly blooms, in a summer berry mix of pinks, magenta, and purples, with rich veining and
dark come-hither eyes. The Tumbelina, Frills and Spills, and Sweet Sunshine ranges are
slightly more sophisticated, and a tad more subtle with some unusual colours, blends, and
veining. Some have a delicate sweet clove-like fragrance. All are smartly compact
and adorable.

Multifloras and millifloras. These petunias are mounding, compact, and particularly free-flowering. Perfect for mass planting in traditional beds and borders, with good weather tolerance, and they produce a floriferous and uniform display. *Petunia multiflora* Shock Wave has small flowers and spreads naturally to produce very tightly packed floriferous baskets and containers that recover well after summer showers. To create a tight carpet effect, look for the *P. multiflora* Frenzy series or 'QT' ("quality tunia") multifloras. The charming Picobella and Minitunia series are millifloras in really fun colours and unusual blends.

Novelties. New novelty petunias are possibly the most fun and slightly crazy varieties that have ever dared to bloom, and they're coming soon to a hanging basket near you. Petunia breeders are trying to develop ever more curious, extraordinary, and striking hybrids. There's been a big trend for black and deep dark novelty types. I love them, and one of the best petunia displays I've seen was a huge basket planted up with just one petunia, 'Black Velvet Improved'. Grown to perfection, it looked bold, beautiful, and dramatic. I also love black stripy 'Phantom' and 'Pinstripe'.

Potunia and Potunia Plus are exciting ranges of bold and unusual varieties. 'Potunia Plus Purple' is a rich claret wine, 'Potunia Purple Halo' is an angelic bicolour (white and purple), and 'Potunia Plus Soft Pink Morning' has a pale lemony green eye that bleeds into light pink.

The Cascadias, Corona, and Rim series often feature a strikingly contrasting edge all the way around the rim of the bloom. 'Cascadias Indian Summer' is mutable, opening a golden yellow, blushing through apricot and peach, and ending as a pale terracotta orange.

The Peppy series are early flowering star-patterned varieties that have differing degrees of stripes or ripples along the length of the large funnel-like flowers.

The Crazytunia series holds the most quirky and extraordinary hybrids of all. Colour combinations that defy nature and the colour wheel all in one. I'm strangely drawn to the cherry red and clotted cream striped madness of 'Crazytunia Cherry Cheesecake' and an ever-increasing list of others.

Phlox

HERBACEOUS ANNUAL FOR BORDERS / POTS / WINDOW BOXES

Phlox drummondii and its cultivars offer pretty clusters of starry summer flowers in a fantastic colour range on short sturdy stems. Often the individual blooms have a distinct central eye in a different colour or deeper or subtly paler shade. These are robust, charming plants, and the newest hybrids flower for months. Do give them a go. Grow from seed (bottom heat). Cut back and feed after flowering.

The 21st Century series is hard to beat, vigorous showy little F1 hybrids in a terrific range of colours. Two creamy pastel ranges to really hunt out are the wonderfully named *Phlox drummondii* 'Phlox of Sheep', in soft rhubarb, custard, and peach melba pastels, and the even paler *P. drummondii* 'Crème Brûlée', whose unusual bicolours have a more gentle vintage feel. The Intensia series contains quite new and vigorous drummondii-derived hybrids in pinks and white; 'Intensia Cabernet' is a deep magenta with a dark eye, and 'Intensia Orchid Blast' a paler pink with a glowing neon centre. Both bordering on orgasmic. Popstars is a mix of short compact selections of *P. drummondii*, with spiky eyelash-petalled flowers in all sorts of light and dark bicolours.

Phormium *(New Zealand flax)*

EVERGREEN PERENNIAL FOR BORDERS / POTS

Phormiums are a year-round presence; they make great specimen plants, helping to focus or anchor a border or container display, or to tie the two together. Their tough leathery sword-like leaves, which come in various colours, bring a different dimension and movement to bedding, in a way that is similar to but bolder than grasses and sedges. Propagate by division. Plants can rot at the base after heavy frosts in wet harsh winters. Use a thick dry mulch like gravel around the crown. Plants tolerate wind, but leaves can split and look tatty, so shelter is best.

Phormium cookianum subsp. *hookeri* 'Cream Delight', an AGM plant, and the hybrid 'Yellow Wave' are favourites; both have very pale creamy yellow variegation. Of the many other hybrids, 'Platt's Black' is the darkest of the bronze and burgundy forms, with a strappy feel to the foliage; 'Jester' and 'Evening Glow' have particularly red-pink foliage; and 'Maori Queen' has darker olive to grey-green leaves with even brighter red stripes.

Plectranthus
(Swedish ivy / spur flower)

☼ ☀

EVERGREEN PERENNIAL FOR BORDERS
/ POTS / HANGING BASKETS /
WINDOW BOXES

Plectranthus is a large genus of well over three hundred species, many of them worth bedding out for their diverse leaf shapes, colours, and textures. Overall they are slightly more substantial than but otherwise quite similar to coleus (*Solenostemon*)—perfect plants for adding extra dramatic foliage texture to border and container displays, in other words. Some have pretty spikes of delicate tubular flowers, but I grow them just for their amazing leaves. Propagate from softwood cuttings. Most will grow well in dappled shade, but the brighter the location, the better the foliage colours. Harden off and pinch out to keep compact.

Plectranthus madagascariensis 'Variegated Mintleaf', which is very easily propagated, is a hugely popular foliage plant for hanging baskets and containers; it has a pleasant prostrate habit, and its slightly succulent mint-scented apple green leaves, edged in creamy white, look great with white and pale pastel blooms. *Plectranthus argentatus* 'Silver Shield' is sturdy, large-leaved, and upright, with some of the thickest, most velvety silver foliage you'll ever encounter. *Plectranthus fruticosus* 'James' is another upright shrubby type with rich green heart-shaped leaves, softly hairy and toothed, and purple-tinged stems. 'Cerveza 'n Lime' is a wonderful felty-leaved acid green aromatic hybrid that can be kept tight and compact with lots of pinching out.

Plumbago (Cape leadwort)

EVERGREEN PERENNIAL FOR BORDERS / POTS

The pale baby boy blue of the clusters of the phlox-like flowers of *Plumbago auriculata* are unique. This is a tough shrubby plant from South Africa that you will sometimes see grown as a hedge in warm frost-free gardens. As an elegant arching specimen in a border or container, it's something rather special. A very pretty conservatory plant for much cooler climates, too. 'Escapade Blue' is a popular pale blue selection; 'Royal Cape' is a slightly deeper blue. I adore f. *alba* (an AGM) and 'Escapade White', too—incredibly delicate and for me just as special as the blues. Propagate from seed (bottom heat) or semi-ripe cuttings. Keep frost-free. Trim plants to a tight framework in spring, and new arching shoots will appear. Leaves have a natural white exudate from "chalk" glands on their undersides, not to be confused with mildew.

Portulaca
(moss rose / Mexican rose)

SUCCULENT ANNUAL FOR BORDERS / POTS / HANGING BASKETS / WINDOW BOXES

Portulaca grandiflora hybrids are trailing and spreading succulents with small but thick and fleshy leaves and fruity bright flowers reminiscent of rock roses. They come in mouthwateringly tropical colours and bright white. Ideally they need lots of hot weather and well-drained soil to show off and sizzle in the sun. Grow from seed (bottom heat). Plants will tolerate thin poor sandy soils, but add some organic matter when planting to help them establish.

The semi-doubles in the Happy Hour and Happy Trails series are early into flower, well branched, and come in zingy hues and white. I love the simple single flower types, too. The Mojave series offers great drought-tolerant groundcovers, some with fried-egg-yolk yellow centres; 'Mojave Tangerine', with its apricot orange petals and brick red eye, is a stunner.

Primula

HERBACEOUS PERENNIAL FOR BORDERS / POTS / WINDOW BOXES

I simply can't get enough of colourful bedding primulas (primroses and polyanthus). They are mostly hybrids, derived originally from crosses made between primroses (*Primula vulgaris*), oxlips (*P. elatior*), cowslips (*P. veris*), and a few other *Primula* species. The brilliant clusters of flowers emerge amongst the leaves, sometimes each bloom on its own short pedicle or clustered around the top of a taller main stem. These plants provide some of the boldest (and lowest) spring colour in cooler temperate regions, and every spring I fall in love with them all over again, from old-favourite cultivars to brand-new introductions. Propagate by seed or division; many varieties will last from one year to the next and are easy to grow on and divide.

Belarina is a series of fully double primulas, and some varieties have delightful little green collars of leaves around the individual flowers, which makes them even more adorable. 'Francisca' has clusters of frilly Granny Smith apple green flowers, with egg-custard middles—an unusual lime hybrid that I totally adore. 'Delia Woodland Dell' is a compact hybrid with all sorts of pale candy pink, lilac, and lavender blooms and good dark green foliage. For very bright red, orange, and yellow blends and bicolours, look for *Primula* ×*polyantha* 'Fire', 'Fire Dragon', and 'Firecracker'.

The Stella series offers hardy, free-flowering, and utterly brilliant polyanthus with gorgeous dark green to bronze foliage. 'Stella Champagne' is a wonderful mix of apricot, pinks, and pale yellows, and the flowers of 'Stella Regal Red' and 'Stella Neon Violet' have a very small yellow eye and rich deep velvety petals.

If the words "rosebud" and "frilly"' get you a tiny bit overexcited (me too) then look for the Primlet or Petticoat series, available in the most dreamy range of colours. These are miniature rosebud primulas, and some have a slight sweet scent. 'Cupid Lemon' is a gorgeous rosebud variety.

Polyanthus in the attractive Gold-laced and Silver-laced Groups have a slightly formal Victorian auricula feel. Bright egg-yolk-centred blooms with dark burgundy black petals that have a thick golden or silver edge, respectively. Smart eye-catching classics.

At the other end of the bright and bold spectrum is *Primula vulgaris*, the British native primrose. An excellent, tough-as-old-boots garden plant with beautiful scent and delicate soft pale creamy blooms. Hard to beat the understated original, but *P. vulgaris* 'Dunbeg' has the softest pale pink flowers against rich bronze leaves. It's from the very hardy Kennedy Irish series, just one of the great ranges of dark-leaved primulas to look for.

Rudbeckia
(black-eyed susan)

☼ ☼

HERBACEOUS ANNUAL OR BIENNIAL
FOR BORDERS / POTS

Rudbeckia hirta and its cultivars are the annual or biennial types brilliant for bedding out. Hybrids are often tetraploids with large flowerheads; they can be doubles or have attractive markings on the outer ray florets. All are truly glorious summer daisies. Drink them in: the memory of their display will keep your spirit warm through the most miserable of winters. Fun but sometimes a little floppy, so have some brushwood in place for staking. Easy from seed (bottom heat). Plants enjoy quite rich heavy soils but must be well drained.

Rudbeckia hirta 'Chim Chiminee' is an unusual quilled-petalled mix in rustic tones. The Toto range offers tidily compact but floriferous selections with chocolate noses, perfect for containers. 'Caramel Mix' is my favourite range of single, double, and semi-double hybrids in a subtle range of autumnal shades: apricot pink, butterscotch, toffee—all sorts of delicious tones.

Rudbeckia hirta 'Prairie Sun' and 'Irish Eyes' are tall singles with bright two-tone lemon yellow and gold petals and lime green cones; 'Maya' is a golden fully double compact teddy bear. 'Cappuccino' blooms have rich mahogany orange centres and golden petals, 'Cherry Brandy' is a deep velvety burgundy red, and 'Tiger Eye Gold', 'Marmalade', and 'Indian Summer' are solid reliable simple golden daisy selections.

Salvia

EVERGREEN PERENNIAL OR ANNUAL
FOR BORDERS / POTS / WINDOW BOXES

I adore salvias—so many wonderful plants from which to choose. Most traditional for bedding out are the short scarlets of *Salvia splendens*, but *S. patens* and *S. farinacea* and their cultivars are happy to add their silvers, blues, purples, and mauves to the scheme.

I like the much taller more substantial cultivars and new improved tetraploid hybrids, grown as specimens on their own or in container combinations. More and more I'm also growing the shrubby, smaller-flowering super-floriferous types in patio pots. Many are hybrids (*S. ×jamensis*) involving *S. microphylla* and *S. greggii*, both drought- and heat-tolerant shrubby Mexican species. Most can be trimmed back to a short framework after flowering, and in no time they are smothered in blooms again. *Salvia nemorosa* and *S. coccinea* types, which bees and other pollinators adore, should also be considered for displays. All in all, it's a very diverse group of half-hardy plants brilliant for bedding out. Grow from seed or cuttings (softwood or semi-ripe). Pinch out tips to get well-branched shrubby plants.

Salvia patens 'Patio Deep Blue' is short (30 cm, 12 in.), compact, and well branched, carrying striking true-blue hooded florets on erect stems above lovely felty toothed foliage; 'Blue Angel' is an intense blue compact selection and readily available as seed. *Salvia nemorosa* 'Blue Marvel' has the largest flowers of all selections of that species and is a reliable rebloomer to boot.

Salvia farinacea 'Blue Frost' and 'Fairy Queen' both have large deep blue flowers with a white blotch on the bottom lip. The Victoria and Seascape series offer reliable, uniform, early-flowering selections in silvers, blues, purples, and bicolours. 'Mystic Spires Blue' is an impressive hybrid with thick large purple-blue flower spikes.

Easy from seed, the compact selections of *Salvia coccinea* that constitute the Summer Jewel series are quick to bloom and make neat and tidy plants with scented foliage. 'Brenthurst' and shorter 'Coral Nymph' are gorgeous shell pink selections.

Salvia greggii 'Radio Red' and 'Furman's Red' are adored by hummingbirds and butterflies. For an equally ravishing and attractive crimson, try *S. ×jamensis* 'Red Velvet'. *Salvia* 'Hot Lips', an AGM, is a flirty red and white bicolour, whose flowers can go all red or all white in the summer months, thanks to the warmer night temperatures, but will often return to their full bicoloured brilliance in autumn. *Salvia* 'Love and Wishes' is a super-floriferous perennial with rich raspberry purple flowers and dark burgundy calyces and stems. A real head-turner. Finally, 'Wendy's Wish' fulfils my intense need for hits of deepest magenta flowers in late summer; the calyces are a dusky rose colour and the stems, beetroot. Grow this hybrid as an annual.

Sanvitalia
(Mexican creeping zinnia)

ANNUAL FOR BORDERS / POTS / HANGING BASKETS / WINDOW BOXES

If you like the endless symmetry of daisies, you may just love *Sanvitalia procumbens*—a pretty, low, spreading plant covered in tiny golden blooms that trails from pots and baskets, plays amongst taller plants, or bumbles over the edges of beds, borders, and paths. Adorable. *Sanvitalia procumbens* 'Orange Sprite' has a teeny-tiny sunflower look; each flower has yellow-orange petals and a dark black-brown eye. 'Sunbini' is a floriferous, bright warm yellow hybrid with golden green centres, healthy fresh green foliage, and a tight compact habit. 'Gold Crown' is a rich yellow hybrid. Grow from seed (bottom heat). Plants will tolerate poor sandy soils, but enrich with organic matter when planting to help them establish.

Scabiosa *(scabious / pincushion flower)*

ANNUAL OR PERENNIAL FOR BORDERS / POTS / WINDOW BOXES

Pincushion, powder-puff, or anemone-type blooms are yet another obsession of mine. No wonder I adore scabious. *Scabiosa atropurpurea* (sweet scabious) and its bushy selections are favourites, as they come in the most wonderful range of rich deep berry colours and pastels. There are large-flowered annual forms or short-lived floriferous perennials with feathery medium green leaves and upright branching stems. The darkest sometimes have a subtle scent. I adore the burgundy and blackcurrant seletions 'Burgundy Beau' and 'Black Cat'. Dark and delicious. 'Beaujolais Bonnets' is special, a mix of deep plum centres and paler pink petals. 'Summer Fruits' is a plethora of pink and deep burgundy shades, 'Salmon Pink' is a coral-tinged medium pink, 'Fata Morgana' an unusual apricot, and 'Snowmaiden' a gorgeous pure white. 'Blue Cockade' has some of the biggest flowers. The often slightly shorter, more perennial *S. columbaria* types (e.g., 'Blue Note') also make wonderful patio plants that bees and butterflies adore. Grow from seed (bottom heat); annual types are best sown direct. Trim after flowering to encourage more flowers.

Scaevola *(fairy fan flower)*

PERENNIAL FOR BORDERS / POTS / HANGING BASKETS / WINDOW BOXES

Scaevola aemula is native to coastal Australia, and it and its selections are tough, spreading, mat-forming plants. The blooms are curiously fan-shaped, unusual, and useful in terms of adding to the diversity of flower forms in a display. Robust enough to use as groundcovers and tolerant of salt spray, too. The newest selections are better-branching and more compact, and the colour range now extends to rich pinks, creamy yellows, and stripy pyjama bicolours: look out for 'Zig Zag', a purple and white fandango. The Wonder and Whirlwind series are robust improvements on the straight species in a fantastic range of colours. 'Blue Print' is a standout lavender mauve, and 'Suntastic' a subtle pale primrose with a rich lemon eye. Propagate by layering or softwood cuttings (bottom heat). Trim after flowering, and water with a dilute feed; plants will bounce back quickly.

Solenostemon
(coleus / painted nettle)

EVERGREEN PERENNIAL FOR
BORDERS / POTS / HANGING BASKETS /
WINDOW BOXES

I treasure the extraordinary and kaleidoscopic range of form and colour in the
leaves of coleus, as I still tend to call them.
They are one of the first plants I grew from
seed when I was very little. I still love them, and for providing powerfully showy foliage,
these Victorian favourites are utterly marvellous. Propagate by seed or softwood cuttings,
which will root quickly in warm bright conditions. These are, in fact, one of the easiest plants
to take cuttings of, so consider yourself warned: coleus are totally addictive. Pinch out to
encourage bushy growth.

I have lots of favourites. *Solenostemon scutellarioides* 'Fishnet Stockings' has intricate dark
burgundy black veining across apple green foliage; 'Black Dragon' has velvety, frilly leaves,
edged almost black, with red-pink centres; 'Chocolate Mint' is deep brown with a zesty lime
green edge; 'Chocolate Covered Cherry' is a delicious cherry, burgundy, and lime green
hybrid. The Versa and Wizard series are compact, colourful, and naturally branching and
don't need much pinching out; grow the Kong series for ginormously large, spectacularly
lovely leaves. There are lots of wonderful AGM varieties, too—'China Rose' is a delicious
rich pink and purple; 'Trusty Rusty', red, russet, and gold; 'Redhead', a solid burgundy
maroon; and 'Henna', olive green with rusty red veins and nettle-like extra-serrated edges.

Strobilanthes
(Persian shield / royal purple plant)

EVERGREEN PERENNIAL FOR BORDERS / POTS /
WINDOW BOXES

Strobilanthes dyeriana is a dramatic tropical foliage plant that's
rather special. It has long lanceolate leaves that are a metallic
violet-purple. Stunningly unusual as a shrubby specimen plant and
works a treat, colour-wise, with deep pinks, reds, silvers, and black.
Grow from seed or softwood cuttings. Tender and needs consistent warmth, shelter, and
good sun to thrive. The straight species is more than sufficiently wonderful.

Sutera (bacopa)

EVERGREEN PERENNIAL FOR POTS / HANGING BASKETS / WINDOW BOXES

Sutera cordata is a very dainty and airy filler or spiller perfect for mingling amongst bolder plants in baskets and containers. It has pretty little serrated leaves and tiny star-like flowers. Now that golden-leaved and pink- and mauve-flowering varieties have been developed, it's a much more versatile choice. The double-blooming types are rather winning, too. Propagate by layering or softwood cuttings. Thrives in cool moist locations. A short-lived perennial best grown as an annual. As always, the most robust cultivars are cutting-raised.

Many good whites have arrived, such as the floriferous *Sutera cordata* 'Snowtopia' and the big, clear-flowering hybrids of the Snowstorm series; 'Snowstorm Blue Bubbles' has double lilac mauve flowers. Members of the Scopia series are early to flower with a compact, branched and trailing habit. 'Scopia Double Ballerina Snowball' is a charming double white, and 'Scopia Gulliver Blue' has pale mauve blooms. Abunda varieties are slightly more heat tolerant, have basal branching, and bloom nonstop.

Tagetes (marigold)

ANNUAL FOR BORDERS / POTS / WINDOW BOXES

When it comes to bold, bright delivery of pretty much any tint, tone, or shade of yellow or orange, you can totally rely on marvellous marigolds. The genus *Tagetes* is native to the Americas, chiefly Mexico, but various species have naturalised in countries around the world. Most widely cultivated are the French marigolds, so called because many of the original cultivars were bred in France from *T. patula*. African (or American) marigolds are the taller, truly huge cultivars involving *T. erecta*, with chunky spherical heads. These two key species are used in the breeding of lots of very popular and resilient sterile hybrids, which are often even more floriferous and robust than their parents; these *T. patula* × *T. erecta* crosses are often highlighted as triploids in seed catalogues. Signet marigolds are also popular; they are quite tall, ferny-leaved plants derived mostly from *T. tenuifolia*. Across the different types of marigolds there are different flower forms, too, from simple singles through semi-doubles and fully doubles, as well as crested and anemone forms. Grow from seed (bottom heat). Slugs and snails will demolish young plants, so have protection in place when planting out. The robust triploids keep pumping out blooms whether deadheaded or not. Grow tall types in bright light to avoid floppy lax plants.

French marigolds. French marigolds make brilliant companion plants around the garden because their nectar-rich flowers are adored by hoverflies, whose larvae are aphid-eating machines; flies often lay eggs right next to aphid colonies. My favourites are the very rich rusty red and burnt orange varieties, and there are lots of great ones to choose from. Durango series holds reliable, short, and well-branched selections of *Tagetes patula* that have large blooms with anemone centres. Bonanza series offers early-flowering plants with large crested blooms. 'Alumia Vanilla Cream' is a creamy lemon that's rather unusual. 'Strawberry Blonde' is an excitingly subtle peachy pink. For cutting, I love to grow 'Tall Scotch Prize' or 'Striped Marvel', both with dazzling deep maroon and egg-yolk yellow pyjama-striped flowers; the blooms of 'La Bamba' have two rich tangerine stripes per satsuma yellow petal. All are selections of *T. patula.*

African marigolds. Tagetes erecta 'Vanilla' is an enormous creamy F1, like a cone of ice cream. 'Fantastic Mix' offers tall plants with super-shaggy lion's-mane flowerheads made up of masses of long, narrow, incurved petals clustered together. Blooms come in different shades of orange and yellow.

Triploid marigolds. Zenith is a series of short compact bomb-proof hybrids that need no deadheading and flower relentlessly. Strong, well branched, and floriferous in oranges, reds, and yellows. 'Konstance' has big double mahogany blooms with fiery burning embers on the underside and edges of the petals.

Signet marigolds. Bright starry mounds of tiny single flowers, perfect for edging paths, as the citrus-scented foliage fills the air as you brush past. Plant among your tomatoes, too, to increase bee activity. *Tagetes tenuifolia* 'Golden Gem' is a rich orange, and 'Lemon Gem' is a neat hybrid signet smothered in a haze of zingy citrus flowers. 'Gem Mixed' is a reliable mixture of colours.

Thunbergia
(black-eyed susan vine)

☀

PERENNIAL FOR BORDERS / POTS

Thunbergia alata and its cultivars are attractive climbing perennial vines usually grown as annuals. Plants have thin twining stems with arrowhead-shaped leaves. The flowers have five petals and are typically orange or yellow with a jet black throat at the centre. These are useful vigorous plants for quickly covering a fence or trellis or to make a temporary screen. You can plant them as a groundcover, but to truly appreciate them, let them scramble up a support or structure of some sort. Grow from seed (bottom heat). Soak seeds in warm water overnight to speed up germination, and press the seeds into compost in individual pots. Tiny pinhead-sized red spider mites on the undersides of leaves can cause unsightly webbing and yellow mottled foliage. To control, spray plants with dilute organic insecticidal soap on dull days, when bee activity is low.

I like the white forms best—'Alba' or 'Susie White Black Eye'. A pure white flower with such a jet black eye is really quite rare. 'Pure White' has a very pale lime green eye. 'Susie Mix' includes orange, yellow, and white flowers, with and without contrasting dark eyes. For big bright tangerine trumpets, go for 'Orange Beauty'; 'African Sunset' has flowers in fiery terracotta and apricot coral; 'Lemon A-Peel' and 'Lemon' are zingy citrus yellows with black centres. All are selections of bright eyes, another of *Thunbergia alata*'s common names.

Tiarella (foam flower)

☀ ☀

RHIZOMATOUS HERBACEOUS PERENNIAL FOR BORDERS / POTS / WINDOW BOXES

Like heucheras and heucherellas, tiarellas are delightful perennials that come into their own in displays in slightly cooler shadier locations. Their tiny star-shaped flowers on erect stems are like mini-fairywands above pretty mounds of palmately lobed leaves that have all sorts of delicate markings and variegation. I adore the many very pretty hybrids with variegated leaves. Favourites include 'Mystic Mist' and 'Skid's Variegated', which are pale lime and creamy white speckled forms that turn pinkish in the autumn. 'Pink Skyrocket' has very impressive erect wands of pink and white flowers above good deep green leaves with chocolatey centres, and 'Iron Butterfly' is a classic with bronze chocolate finger-like veining on rich green lobed leaves. Propagate by seed or division. Plants can rot in excessively wet winters. Keep in a sheltered dry spot.

Torenia (wishbone flower)

HERBACEOUS ANNUAL FOR BORDERS / POTS / HANGING BASKETS / WINDOW BOXES

Torenia fournieri hybrids are versatile, filling in and spilling out of containers and good as an annual groundcover in a border. Plants have simple fresh glossy green leaves with serrated edges and pretty foxglove-like flowers that have a fun sweet-shop feel and yellow throat markings. Grow from seed (bottom heat). Torenias can be good alternatives to impatiens in warm, sheltered, semi-shady spots. They grow best in moist soils in dappled sunlight. Butterflies and hummingbirds love them, but thankfully deer and rabbits don't.

The Clown mix of compact varieties has licks and splotches of bright yellow on the lips of the purple, plum, pink, and white blooms. The Moon series—bigger, more vigorous cascading plants—is good for large hanging baskets and pots; 'Moon Yellow' with its plum purple throat is rather striking, as is candy pink 'Moon Rose'. The Summer Wave series has some of the biggest blooms; go for these, especially if you love purples, blues, and mauves. Catalina hybrids have quite large blooms, perform well in shady locations, and come in a great range of colours; 'Catalina Grape-O-Licious' is white with an occasional pale lemon lick and a violet eye that winks at you. A versatile series for pots, baskets, and groundcover, too.

Trifolium (clover)

HERBACEOUS PERENNIAL FOR BORDERS / POTS / HANGING BASKETS / WINDOW BOXES

I love the oversized creamy white flowers of *Trifolium ochroleucon* (sulphur clover), as do foraging bees and butterflies, and I've been totally drawn in by the unusual-leaved selections of *T. repens* (white clover, Dutch clover): 'Dragon's Blood' has feathery burgundy markings down the central leaf veins on silvery blue-green leaves; 'Purpurascens' and 'Atropurpureum' have chocolatey burgundy blotched leaves with apple green edges and either white or pink flowers; and 'William' has ruby pink flowers and leaflets that start green at the centre and then turn to maroon halfway towards the edge. Gorgeous. Such useful, tough, spreading plants; and their classic trifoliate leaves, made up of three tiny leaflets, are perfection itself. Great as groundcovers on moist soils and also cascading out of containers. Propagate by layering, division, or softwood cuttings. These are quick-to-root plants: you can literally break off a section of stem and shove it into the soil. After flowering, trim hard to encourage a crop of fresh new foliage.

Tropaeolum (nasturtium)

HERBACEOUS ANNUAL FOR BORDERS / POTS / HANGING BASKETS / WINDOW BOXES

Nasturtiums (*Tropaeolum majus*) are the first flowers I grew at primary school. They are that blooming easy and have to be one of the most rewarding plants to grow, with their cheery flowers, roundish leaves, and big spherical seeds that are hard to miss and easy to handle. All parts are edible, but it's the peppery flowers that taste best. Really vigorous climbing types (e.g., 'Spitfire', 'Indian Chief', 'Crimson Emperor') are great at covering pretty much anything in the garden from fences and walls to large expanses of rough ground. So is *T. peregrinum* (canary creeper), a vigorous yet delicate-looking species from Peru that's just as easy to grow from seed; it has slender stems, pale green leaves, a profusion of feathery yellow Tweetie-Pie flowers—and it will scramble over anything. For smaller bedding displays and containers, choose the more compact free-flowering varieties that make pretty rounded mounding plants. Give all nasturtiums a warm sunny and well-drained position in poorish soils for best flowering; on rich wet soils, plants can grow too exuberantly, and flowers are lost under a sea of lush foliage. Nasturtiums are a food plant for the caterpillars of numerous butterflies and moths, and they also serve as an indicator plant for blackfly aphids, as they are among the first plants to attract these pests. Grow from seed or stem-tip softwood cuttings.

Of the dwarf nasturtiums, I love the many that offer rich opulent shades, including *Tropaeolum majus* 'Tom Thumb'. Alaska series is the classic marble-leaved type, with selections flowering in a great range of colours. Troika series was bred for baskets and containers, but these "tumbling" floriferous selections of *T. majus* do well in borders, too. 'Just Peachy', a soft apricot selection with pale lime green leaves, looks great in combination with bronze- and dark-leaved neighbours. 'Fruit Salad' is a bicoloured hybrid with attractive serrated petals. *Tropaeolum majus* 'Cherry Rose Jewel' is refreshing—an unusual rich pinky red that's quite eye-poppingly good.

Tulipa *(tulip)*

PERENNIAL BULB FOR BORDERS / POTS / WINDOW BOXES

For me, tulips are the divas of any spring bedding display. It's such a treat to see the earliest of them starting the parade, flaunting their glorious rainbow colours against those first bright blue skies as the garden gets into the spring swing of things. Different flower forms and flowering times are something to consider if you want a continuous and ever-evolving display. For low-growing early-flowering tulips, choose certain species tulips, the gregii and kaufmanniana types, and early doubles; these are perfect for containers and window boxes. For really big bowl-shaped flouncy types, look for *Tulipa fosteriana* and early singles, as well as *T. praestans* and multi-headed tulips, which are often more midseason. Later-flowering tulips include many of the lily-flowered, viridiflora, parrot, and double-late peony forms. Most of all, my advice is to go mad in autumn and plant bucketsful in beds, borders, and containers. Plant slightly deeper than other bulbs, ideally three times the length of the bulb, from late autumn to early winter. Stagger and scatter your choices, and these bulbs will fill your boots with pure joyous colour for weeks.

I'm always led by colour, so this dictates my absolute favourites. For peach and apricot I adore early-flowering 'Apricot Beauty' and 'La Belle Époque'. Gentle soft pink favourites include 'Angélique' and 'Pink Diamond'; deeper pink favourites are 'Royal Acres', 'Paradise Island', 'Gipsy Love', 'The Cure', and 'Mariette'. For white and cream, I adore 'Ivory Floradale' and lily-flowered 'White Triumphator'. My list of deepest dark plum to blackberry favourites grows ever longer with 'Café Noir', 'Antraciet', 'Burgundy', and 'Black Hero'. 'Aladdin' is just one of the many good reds, but early and short 'Red Riding Hood' is truly excellent. Orange favourites include sublimely scented 'Ballerina' and 'Orange Emperor'. For tulips with green flushes and streaks, look to the wonderful viridifloras. All wonderfully fresh and unusual. And my top yellow variety is lily-flowered 'West Point'. Exquisite.

Verbena

PERENNIAL FOR BORDERS / POTS /
HANGING BASKETS / WINDOW BOXES

Verbenas are brilliantly floriferous and totally versatile plants. *Verbena bonariensis*, a tall upright species beloved by bees and butterflies, is phenomenally popular in borders, and now, shorter compact selections good for containers are available, too—look for 'Little One' and 'Lollipop'.

Verbena rigida is a semi-hardy tuberous perennial (often treated as an annual) that deserves to be grown more widely, ideally in fertile but very sharply draining soils and sunny open locations. It is very floriferous and produces glorious candelabras of rich purple flowers. Forma *lilacina* 'Polaris' is a gorgeous greyish lilac and 'Santos Purple' a super-rich violet selection, but the straight species is hard to beat.

Particularly glorious for bedding out are the hybrid garden verbenas (*Verbena ×hybrida*), which are available in an amazing range of colours. Some have flowers with tiny white eyes, some come in rich solid hues, and others have flowerheads full of tiny florets at different stages of maturity, resulting in an incredible display of subtle tones and shades. They can look classy and eye-catching on their own in a simple terracotta pot, or work brilliantly well weaving through other plants in borders, container plantings, and hanging baskets. They will flower right up until hard frosts and can be kept going even longer in a frost-free conservatory. I can't get enough of them. The Quartz series is widely available and comes in a great range of colours. I'm slightly giddy about the Bebop series, verbenas whose sugary sweet bicoloured flowers have little white eyes. 'Bebop Pink' is pure Barbie Doll. 'Peaches 'n' Cream' is the ultimate apricot, reminiscent of '70s bridesmaid dresses; teamed with rich bronze and chocolatey brown foliage, it looks rather modern and marvellous. 'Sissinghurst' is a dependable classic rich pink with gorgeous grey-green foliage.

Verbena bonariensis and *V. rigida* are easy to grow from seed; the hybrid bedding verbenas are best from softwood cuttings. Powdery mildew can be a challenge with all three types of these gorgeous plants, so space them well and have a bicarbonate-based organic spray at the ready. If the disease is particularly troublesome in your garden, grow mildew-resistant varieties. The Aztec, Superbena, and Rapunzel series contain some good mildew-resistant hybrids.

Viola

ANNUAL OR PERENNIAL FOR BORDERS
/ POTS / HANGING BASKETS / WINDOW
BOXES

The range of violas is vast. The larger-flowering types are commonly called pansies, and those with smaller flowers, violas, but most are simply complex hybrids within the genus *Viola*. Often the biggest selection can be found in nurseries and garden centres, for planting from mid autumn through winter and into early spring. There are semi-trailing types suitable for hanging baskets, and all sorts of fun and colourful novelties, too. As well as the popular bedding types grown as hardy annuals or biennials, there are perennial violas that will keep going from one year to the next but are best regularly refreshed, trimmed back, and propagated by cuttings. Propagate from seed or stem-tip softwood cuttings. Deadhead to prolong flowering. Cut back hard after flowering to keep compact. Water with a balanced dilute liquid feed, and plants will quickly reshoot.

Bedding pansies. Pansies (often *Viola* ×*wittrockiana* hybrids) have much bigger, more rounded flowers. They are larger, taller, less compact plants than violas. They are available in pretty much every colour and combination you can imagine. Plain types are one pure colour across the whole bloom; bicolours feature two distinct colours or tones. The classic varieties have either a "face" (a dark central blotch of black) or "whiskers" (fine black stripes radiating from the centre).

Matrix is a reliable *Viola* ×*wittrockiana* F1 series that comes in a very wide range of colours, some with faces and whiskers but also plain and bicolours. Another is Mystique; its hybrids flower a little later than Matrix, but they are big blooms in an interesting range of colours. If you want full-on frilly pansy style, there are novelties with showy ruffled petals: look out for the Frizzle Sizzle series. *Viola* ×*wittrockiana* 'Chalon Supreme Wildberry' is pure pansy sauciness—Moulin Rouge cancan-skirt blooms in wine, plum purple, and burgundy. Ridiculously good.

Cool Wave is a floriferous series of semi-trailing branching pansies with slightly smaller blooms, great for hanging baskets, window boxes, and containers. 'Cool Wave Lemon Blueberry' is a particularly good blue and yellow bicolour, along with icy blue and white 'Cool Wave Frost'.

Bedding violas. Bedding violas are compact—smaller, shorter, and altogether more dainty and perky than pansies. But they are just as determined to flower their socks off for as long as possible, and if you deadhead them scrupulously they will flower for months. Most are complex hybrids.

Teardrops is a semi-trailing floriferous F1 range that is particularly good for hanging baskets, but the Sorbet and improved Sorbet XP series of F1 hybrids are my favourites and very hard to beat. An incredible range of colours, bicolours, faces, and whiskers—all cheery, sprightly, and uniform; they perform well in containers and in the garden, too. I love cream and blue 'Sorbet XP Coconut Swirl', but it's hard not to feel the same about the colourful little faces of every single variety.

Perennial violas. More and more, these are the violas I'm choosing for my displays. Some have gorgeous scent, and most flower continuously from mid spring through summer. The acidic to khaki 'Green Goddess' is rather interesting and unusual. 'Etain' is a beautiful creamy yellow with gentle pale purple margins and a delicious scent. 'Blackout', 'Roscastle Black', and 'Molly Sanderson' are three brilliant velvety blacks. 'Rebecca', 'Columbine', and 'Elaine Quin' are whites with different degrees of splashes, streaks, or frilly margins of mauve and lilac. All are hybrids.

Zantedeschia (calla lily)

☼

RHIZOMATOUS HERBACEOUS PERENNIAL FOR BORDERS / POTS

Calla lilies—the shorter, more compact cousins of the classic tall white arum lily (*Zantedeschia aethiopica*)—are unusual exotic-looking plants. Originally from Africa, they are perfect for infusing bedding displays with a tropical feel. Those encountered in gardens are usually hybrids involving *Z. elliottiana* and *Z. rehmannii*. Most are tender and thrive in really warm moist conditions. Plants have super-bright and colourful showy spathes (specialised petal-like bracts) shaped like a funnel with a central, finger-like spadix, which carries the true flowers. Leaves are lush, lance-, heart-, or spear-shaped, and can have attractive transparent flecks or other maculations. There are so many wonderful varieties, from pure clean colours, some with matching or contrasting throats and spadices, to subtle blends, blushes, and true bicolours. Callafornia series is a standout, holding strong compact plants in every colour you can imagine. 'Neon Amour' and 'Coral Passion' are right up my zingy pink street, and 'Memories' is perhaps the most dramatic with purple-black trumpets and devilish dark foliage, too. Malevolently marvellous. Propagate by division. Feed fortnightly with a high-nitrogen fertiliser when in active growth (above 22°C, 72°F) but withhold feed during flowering. A high-potassium feed (e.g., tomato fertiliser) can be given once a week after flowering. Lift the rhizomes before frosts and store in dry compost at 10–15°C (50–60°F).

Zinnia (Mexican daisy)

ANNUAL FOR BORDERS / POTS / WINDOW BOXES

Bedding zinnias (*Zinnia* ×*hybrida*) are often hybrids involving *Z. elegans*, a species that has classic daisy-like flowerheads, large and solitary, on bristly stems and coarse lanceolate leaves. All late-summer daisies get a warm welcome in my garden, but the incredibly vibrant blooms of zinnias bring the joyous energy of a Mexican fiesta, so are most thoroughly embraced. There are single, semi-double, fully double, and crested flower types, as well as tall large-flowered beauties great for cutting and shorter well-branched bushy varieties. Grow from seed (bottom heat). Plants need a bright open and airy location to thrive. They can suffer from grey mould in cool damp weather or if planted too densely, so space generously and pray for warm sunshine.

The compact Zahara series is bushy, versatile, and floriferous. These selections of *Zinnia marylandica* are great for the border but good in pots, too; they come in both single and double forms and a larger-flowered (XL) range, all in a wide variety of colours. 'Magellan' is a dependable and uniform F1 hybrid mix of semi-doubles in clear bright colours; plants grow to about 40 cm (16 in.) in height. *Zinnia elegans* Giant Double is a mix of the classic large double-flowered zinnias with tall rigid stems, perfect for cutting or a bedding display. *Zinnia elegans* 'Zinderella Lilac' and 'Zinderella Peach' are mixes of mauve, pink, apricot, and peach pompom-crested types; their range of sunset and candy colours is delicious. *Zinnia elegans* 'Tudor' is the most wonderful deep ruffled magenta, and *Z. elegans* 'Cupid' wins my prize for the cutest smallest pompom-like flowers in a mix of colours. 'Aztec Sunset' is a mix of hybrid bicolours in rich reds, oranges, and yellows. Viva Mexico, Viva Zinnias!

further reading

Bird, Richard. 2000. *Annuals and Perennials*. London: Anness.

Clevely, Andi. 1997. *Gardeners' World Pocket Plants Summer Bedding*. London: BBC Worldwide.

——. 2008. *Plants in Pots*. London: Frances Lincoln.

Colborn, Nigel. 1994. *Annuals and Bedding Plants*. London: Conran Octopus.

Cox, Martyn. 2011. *RHS How to Grow Plants in Pots*. London: Dorling Kindersley.

Fish, Martin. 2004. *Collins Practical Gardener: Bedding Plants*. London: HarperCollins.

Gillman, Jeff. 2008. *The Truth About Garden Remedies*. Portland, Oregon: Timber Press.

——. 2008. *The Truth About Organic Gardening*. Portland, Oregon: Timber Press.

Hessayon, D. G. 2007. *The Bedding Plant Expert*. London: Expert Books.

Lloyd, Christopher. 2001. *Christopher Lloyd's Garden Flowers*. London: Cassell & Co.

——. 2005. *Succession Planting for Adventurous Gardeners*. London: BBC Books.

Miller, Diana. 1996. *Pelargoniums*. London: B. T. Batsford Ltd.

Phillips, Roger, and Martyn Rix. 1999. *Annuals and Biennials*. London: Macmillan.

Rice, Graham. 1986. *A Handbook of Annuals and Bedding Plants*. Portland, Oregon: Timber Press.

——. mygarden.rhs.org.uk/blogs/graham_rice.

Rosenfeld, Richard. 2007. *RHS Containers for Patios*. London: Dorling Kindersley.

Titchmarsh, Alan. 2009. *How to Garden: Container Gardening*. London: BBC Books.

——. 2012. *How to Garden: Instant Colour*. London: BBC Books.

acknowledgements

Many thanks must go to Stuart Lowen and Tiernach McDermott at Ball Colegrave; Michael Perry at Thompson & Morgan; and all the dedicated staff at Birmingham City Parks and Nurseries. Special love and thanks to Norma Vernon, my mum, who shares, supports, and encourages my love of all things floral. This book is dedicated to my much-loved and much-missed granddad, Arthur Worrall, a brilliant plantsman and loving grandfather.

index

about the author

Matthew Kidd

Andy Vernon, author of *The Plant Lover's Guide to Dahlias,* is an award-winning gardening writer, photographer, television producer/director, and RHS horticultural advisor. He is a self-confessed flower fanatic, his love of floriferous displays dating back to the 1970s, when his granddad Arthur Worrall, a passionate plantsman, taught him how to take cuttings of pelargoniums. Andy lives in Cheshire in the United Kingdom with his partner, Matthew, his beloved Jack Russells, Daisy and Percy, and Lulu, his Chihuahua cross. Catch up with him at facebook.com/TheFlowerPoweredGarden.